5-PHASE PROJECT MANAGEMENT

JOSEPH W. WEISS, Ph.D., *Bentley College*

ROBERT K. WYSOCKI, Ph.D., *The TMS Group*

5-PHASE PROJECT MANAGEMENT

A PRACTICAL PLANNING & IMPLEMENTATION GUIDE

ADDISON-WESLEY PUBLISHING COMPANY

Reading, Massachusetts • Menlo Park, California • New York • Don Mills, Ontario
Wokingham, England • Amsterdam • Bonn • Sydney • Singapore • Tokyo
Madrid • San Juan • Paris • Seoul • Milan • Mexico City • Taipei

The publisher offers discounts on this book when ordered in quantity for special sales. For more information please contact:

Corporate & Professional Publishing Group
Addison-Wesley Publishing Company
One Jacob Way
Reading, Massachusetts 01867

Library of Congress Cataloging-in-Publication Data

Weiss, Joseph W.
    5-phase project management : a practical planning & implementation
guide / by Joseph W. Weiss, Robert K. Wysocki.
       p.   cm.
    Includes bibliographical references (p.   ) and index.
    ISBN 0-201-56316-9 (pbk. : acid-free paper)
    1. Industrial project management.   I. Wysocki, Robert K.
II. Title.   III. Title: Five-phase project management.
    HD69.P75W46   1992
    658.4'04—dc20   91-42548
                                          CIP

Cover design by Joyce C. Weston
Text design by Wilson Graphics & Design (Kenneth J. Wilson)
Set in 10 point Palatino by Shepard Poorman Communications Corporation

ISBN 0-201-56316-9

Printed on recycled and acid-free paper.
3 4 5 6 7 8 9 10-CRW-97969594
Third Printing, May 1994

CONTENTS

Preface

WHO NEEDS PROJECT MANAGEMENT METHODS?

If you have to complete work that involves multiple priorities, complex and numerous tasks, deadlines, constant communication across organizational boundaries, limited resources, and do all of this with little if any precedents or guidelines, then you could benefit from using project management techniques. On the other hand, you may have managed projects but feel the need for a refresher course.

Professionals use project management techniques. Engineers in technology firms use project management methods to design and repair hardware and software products. Hospital administrators and their staffs use project management for scheduling purposes. Wholesalers, retailers, and distributors use project management for inventory control. Writers, publishers, and corporate educational staffs use project management for curriculum and manuscript development, as well as marketing planning. The military and government agencies use these methods for designing and manufacturing weapons, space, and other complex systems. Construction contractors use project management in building construction. Executive secretaries often have good reason to use the methods in creating and implementing programs. You can use project management methods to build a house or a boat, to write a novel, or to plan a vacation.

Unfortunately, many of the professionals who use project management techniques do so in partial, fragmented, and sometimes uninformed ways. It is commonplace in our training and consulting to hear seasoned, career professionals admit, "I wish I had known about these techniques and methods 10 years ago. My job would have been much easier."

WHAT TECHNIQUES DOES THIS BOOK OFFER?

In this book we offer a 5-phase approach consisting of 25 action steps, which enables you to define, plan, organize, control, and close a project. Even if you do not direct the project, this approach informs you about the "big picture" of project management, the vocabulary, and the techniques. The elements of project management which we systematically and straightforwardly present include: initial planning, goal and objective setting, identification of work that has to be done, estimating the time and labor to complete work, budgeting the work, implementing the project, controlling and documenting the work, managing people on the project, and finally, closing the project.

Our aim is to empower you with a practical understanding of basic project management techniques; and to enable you to use this book as a guide for briefings and training, to distribute to others who will work on the project, and to revise and add to the checklists and documentation herein to solve your particular problems. To meet this aim, we have chosen three criteria for our selection and presentation of concepts and techniques:

1. Introduce one method with a phased approach that is easy, understandable, and quick to grasp.

2. Select and explain key concepts and techniques that can be used by hand (and with software).

3. Empower and encourage you to plan and initiate a project after reading this book; or, if you are working on a project, to increase your effectiveness on that project.

WHY WE WROTE *5-PHASE PROJECT MANAGEMENT*

We wrote this book as a ready reference to help people in any industry or profession plan and manage projects with limited budgets, time demands, deadlines, and resource constraints. Our aim is to simplify the application of project management techniques through a systematic method with easy-to-use checklists and tips for anyone who must get complex work done on time, within budget, and according to specifications (the golden rule of project management).

With over 15 years each of corporate and administrative consulting, training, and college teaching experience in which we have used project management, we understand the value of having a practical method and user-friendly technique. We also want the book to be what the subtitle states, a practical planning and implementation guide. If the book helps equip you with a method, concepts, vocabulary, and tools that get you going, give you confidence, and increase your boldness and success in applying the content to get project work done on time, within budget, and by specifications, then we will have succeeded.

Our aim is to give you a solid working knowledge of an extremely powerful yet simple-to-use tool that is guaranteed to improve your effectiveness as a manager of both projects and people. After all, your success as a project manager will be measured by your ability to get the job done on time, within budget, and according to specifications.

THE USE OF 5-PHASE PROJECT MANAGEMENT

We have organized project management into 25 easy-to-follow steps, around which 10 chapters are sequenced for quick learning and easy reference. We have tried to say a lot in a little space while making our presentation interesting. Figure 1-1, repeated at the start of each chapter, illustrates the 5 phases and 25 steps in the planning and implementation of project management. This is the "big picture." We suggest you use it as a guide.

Part I

PLANNING THE PROJECT

In a sense the most important part of the project is its beginning. It is here that the "die is cast" and either the project is well-conceived and executable within the time and cost constraints specified by senior management or it is an impossible situation doomed to failure before it even begins. This part of the project is not the place to make rash promises in an attempt to be a hero. Rather, it is a time to rationally and thoughtfully approach the initial specifications of the project in order to avoid impossible situations. Remember that once you have agreed to the project goal, management will expect you to deliver.

Chapter 1

INTRODUCTION

Everyone is a project manager, but not everyone knows how to plan and manage a project. Projects vary in size and scope from a NASA space shuttle launch to building a boat, planning a wedding, or getting a degree. People who have to do projects without training usually lack a practical method and a technique for getting the work done effectively and efficiently.

FIRST THINGS FIRST: WHAT IS A PROJECT?

Program, project, task, and work assignment are often confused. It will help us to distinguish these terms from one another. A *project* is defined as having the following characteristics:

- Complex and numerous activities
- Unique—a one-time set of events
- Finite—with a begin and end date
- Limited resources and budget
- Many people involved, usually across several functional areas in the organizations
- Sequenced activities
- Goal-oriented
- End product or service must result

A task or set of work assignments may be done by one or more persons by using a simple "to-do" list. However, it is evident that a task becomes a project when the above factors begin to dominate and overwhelm individuals who become unable to meet deadlines, budgets, and corporate expectations while working alone.

3

A program is different from a project. A *program* is larger in scope and may comprise multiple projects. For example, the United States government has a space program that includes several projects such as the *Challenger* project. A construction company contracts a program to build an industrial technology park with several separate projects.

WHAT IS PROJECT MANAGEMENT?

When we think of the principles of management we usually associate them with the management of people. Those same principles also apply to projects, as we now illustrate.

PLANNING

Planning involves the establishment of clear and precise objectives (and the work activities that will have to take place to accomplish them) in order to reach a final, stated goal. The goal may involve the solution of a problem or the achievement of some state or condition different from the present one.

ORGANIZING

In addition to organizing people, project management includes the assembly of the necessary resources (manpower, materials, and money) for carrying out the work defined in the plan. It also involves the creation of the structure needed to execute the plan.

CONTROLLING

Once the resources are assembled into a cohesive structure, it will be necessary to monitor and maintain that structure as the project progresses. Control also includes the definition and creation of a reporting structure at specified points through the project life cycle. These reports are designed not only as historical records but also as early warnings of situations and occurrences that are outside nominal performance measures.

CHANGE

Once situations have been discovered that require change, the project manager will have to institute that change. As we will discuss in Chapter Nine, project management includes mechanisms for invoking that change.

Project management is therefore seen as a method and a set of techniques based on the accepted principles of management used for planning, estimating, and controlling work activities to reach a desired end result on time, within budget, and according to specification.

To plan and execute a project using these principles we have utilized a 5-phase method. Each method contains specific steps that expand the general process into a detailed set of procedures. The phased method that will serve as a guide to our development of project management is shown in Figure 1-1.

Figure 1-1   THE 5 PHASES AND 25 ACTION STEPS OF THE PROJECT MANAGEMENT LIFE CYCLE

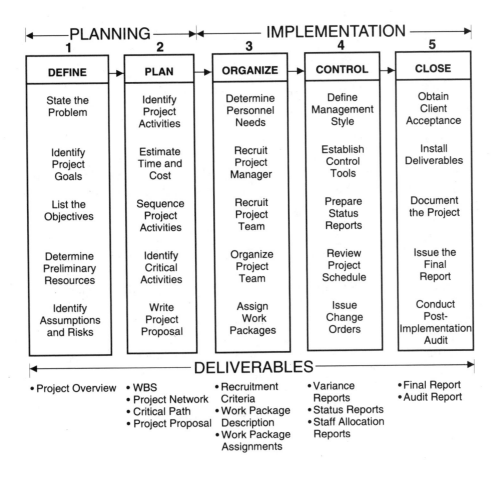

PLANNING		IMPLEMENTATION		
1	2	3	4	5
DEFINE	**PLAN**	**ORGANIZE**	**CONTROL**	**CLOSE**
State the Problem	Identify Project Activities	Determine Personnel Needs	Define Management Style	Obtain Client Acceptance
Identify Project Goals	Estimate Time and Cost	Recruit Project Manager	Establish Control Tools	Install Deliverables
List the Objectives	Sequence Project Activities	Recruit Project Team	Prepare Status Reports	Document the Project
Determine Preliminary Resources	Identify Critical Activities	Organize Project Team	Review Project Schedule	Issue the Final Report
Identify Assumptions and Risks	Write Project Proposal	Assign Work Packages	Issue Change Orders	Conduct Post-Implementation Audit

DELIVERABLES

• Project Overview	• WBS • Project Network • Critical Path • Project Proposal	• Recruitment Criteria • Work Package Description • Work Package Assignments	• Variance Reports • Status Reports • Staff Allocation Reports	• Final Report • Audit Report

TEN MAJOR CAUSES OF PROJECT FAILURE

You do not need to memorize each of the 25 steps in this 5 phase process. These steps help prevent the 10 causes of project failure offered by Danek Bienkowski (1989). Knowing who the "enemy" is gives us a competitive advantage. Projects that follow no method often fail for the following reasons:

1. The project is a solution in search of a problem.

2. Only the project team is interested in the end result.

3. No one is in charge.

4. The project plan lacks structure.

5. The project plan lacks detail.

6. The project is underbudgeted.

7. Insufficient resources are allocated.

8. The project is not tracked against its plan.

9. The project team is not communicating.

10. The project strays from its original goals.

Anyone who has worked on a project has certainly had experiences that would attest to each of these causes. As you read *5-Phase Project Management*, keep these causes in mind and continually ask yourself how they can be avoided.

ADOPTING A PROJECT MANAGEMENT MIND-SET

Our project management approach is a 5-phase method with 25 action steps. It is important to keep in mind at the outset that a project involves more than getting started; it has a life cycle with a beginning, a middle, and an end. The following anecdotal wisdom will serve as a helpful introduction for discussion. These are motivating factors that drive and guide the project management process:

- "Fail to plan; plan to fail."

- "If you don't know where you're going, all roads lead there,"

  or, similarly,

- "If you don't know where you're going, how will you know when you get there?"

- "We may have come here on separate ships, but we're all in the same boat now."

Depending on its size, planning the project can require a substantial commitment of time, energy, and resources. This may be seen as a disadvantage by those not trained or accustomed to having the end product estimated in time, money, people, and effort before beginning. It is an American cultural tradition to start first and think later in product and project development. The Japanese are more adept at spending time and energy gaining consensus before beginning project work. Experience shows that significant waste can occur if adequate planning is not done before a "go" or "no-go" decision to initiate a particular project is carried out. It is important at the outset, then, to develop a frame of mind that takes planning seriously. It is the first step in the process of deciding whether or not to proceed. After the plan is developed, it is the boss. Although the plan is a dynamic and changeable document which involves the input of many individuals, it is still separate from any one person or team and should serve as the cornerstone for driving the project's progress.

It is also important to be goal-directed. Without a project goal that defines and guides all activities and interactions, people and resources go in circles. The goal and objectives are important. Remember, "garbage in, garbage out." Hopefully, the goal statement will be the most valuable milestone.

Finally, project management is not achieved without teamwork. Individuals working alone on complex projects may at times add heroic contributions, but it is as a team that individuals share in the work and glory.

5-PHASE PROJECT MANAGEMENT

	PLANNING		IMPLEMENTATION	
1	**2**	**3**	**4**	**5**
DEFINE	**PLAN**	**ORGANIZE**	**CONTROL**	**CLOSE**
State the Problem	Identify Project Activities	Determine Personnel Needs	Define Management Style	Obtain Client Acceptance
Identify Project Goals	Estimate Time and Cost	Recruit Project Manager	Establish Control Tools	Install Deliverables
List the Objectives	Sequence Project Activities	Recruit Project Team	Prepare Status Reports	Document the Project
Determine Preliminary Resources	Identify Critical Activities	Organize Project Team	Review Project Schedule	Issue the Final Report
Identify Assumptions and Risks	Write Project Proposal	Assign Work Packages	Issue Change Orders	Conduct Post-Implementation Audit

DELIVERABLES

• *Project Overview*	• WBS • Project Network • Critical Path • Project Proposal	• Recruitment Criteria • Work Package Description • Work Package Assignments	• Variance Reports • Status Reports • Staff Allocation Reports	• Final Report • Audit Report

Chapter 2

DEFINING THE PROJECT: THE PROJECT OVERVIEW

In this chapter we focus on producing a document called the *project overview*. It will contain the most valuable information available on the project at this early stage. Beyond being required for the initial "go"/"no-go" decision by management it has a number of other uses. It serves as

1. a general information piece for other managers—keeping others informed is a routine activity in the successful management of projects;

2. an early statement of the goal and direction of the project; and

3. a statement of the problems and opportunities to be addressed by the project.

Once the project is approved for a go-ahead, the project overview becomes the foundation for the more detailed planning activities which follow next. It will serve as the reference base whenever questions or conflicts arise as to future directions for the project. During the early stages of implementation it will be a tool for recruiting and training the project team. Finally, it provides a control point for reporting project progress and an audit point for evaluating the effectiveness of the project in achieving stated goals and objectives. In summary, the project overview will be part of the foundation on which project activities will be based and is a dynamic tool for the ongoing planning and change actions that will surely follow.

STATE THE PROBLEM

As a project manager you must be prepared for a variety of assignments ranging from well-thought-out ones to those that are casually defined by two managers who accidentally meet at the water cooler. The project, yet to be defined, may be clearly outlined in the project overview, what is expected, by when, and with what resources. It will often be accompanied by a written "statement of intent" containing the signatures of the authorizing managers. On the other hand, you have the "water cooler" method, often used to start projects. This type of project is initiated with a vague charge at the water cooler such as, "Bill, I want you to take charge of the annual conference and make sure it doesn't flop like last year's did."

Regardless of which situation you find yourself in, there are specific questions that must be answered before the project begins—even if it begins at the water cooler! Stating and writing a brief description of what the project aims to do is the first step in preparing a project overview statement.

WHAT IS THE PROBLEM/OPPORTUNITY?

A critical need prompts general management to initiate a project management team. The need arises from a problem or situation (internal or external) that either threatens the organization or presents it with a valued opportunity. The need may be for a new product or service, for a new process or system, even for developing new markets; or it may be for cutting back and retrenching a division. The project may involve several professionals from across the organization or only a few people from a single department. The project may require several months or years at great expense or only a few days with little or no incremental costs.

This part of the project overview, as you will see in Figure 2-1 later on, documents not only that need but also the benefit to the organization for undertaking the project. The statement should be short, crisp, and to the point. It should serve as a descriptor for those who although not directly involved on the project may be indirectly involved in supporting the project or simply have a need to be aware that the project is being undertaken. The problem statement, need, opportunity, or benefit can be seen in the example we offer of a conference planning project at the end of this chapter. As we proceed, think about the project you need or want to initiate.

WHAT IS TO BE DONE?

Next, writing the goal of the project follows from stating the problem, the need, and/or the opportunity. This may be a very short but specific statement such as: "Plan and conduct the annual meeting." The important thing to remember is that the goal statement must be phrased using terms that would not mislead anyone who might have reason to read it. It must also use terms that measure its completion. For example, "Write the annual report" is an activity whose completion cannot be measured. On the other hand, "Receive approval of the annual report" is an activity whose completion is known once the approving signature is on the document. The project goal statement is important for two reasons:

1. It is a clear statement of what is to be done.

2. It is an event whose completion can be measured.

Also remember that the project goal directs the course of the entire effort. The goal will be the standard for resolving conflicts, for clarifying expectations, for requesting and justifying resources. The goal is the most important statement initiating the project.

WHO IS RESPONSIBLE FOR THE PROJECT?

There is only one project manager. It is common practice for the authorizing manager to have issued a memo to all parties who might be affected by the project stating the project name, project objective, project manager, and the approximate beginning and ending dates of the project.

Although it is desirable to have the project manager identified at the beginning of the project, it may not be possible in all cases. The person designated may be assigned to another project at some other location in the organization. Or the project manager may have to be hired from outside. As will be discussed later, if the project manager has not been hired at the outset, the requirements of the position can be provided.

WHEN MUST THE PROJECT BE COMPLETED?

This is a critical piece of information. It not only calls attention to the priority that the project will have but also sets in motion a number of planning and budgeting activities. There are two scenarios to consider.

The "Water Cooler" Imposed Deadline

In this case the project deadline was given to the project manager. This may have been the result of a "water cooler" decision, or it may have been imposed because of other factors (customer requirement, your project is part of a larger project, etc.). In any case, as we will show in Chapter Three, you will prepare a plan that shows how the project can be completed by the deadline. In some cases you may have to strive to complete the project by the (sometimes arbitrary) deadline. In other cases (the "water cooler" example), you may be able to negotiate a later deadline, or more resources to meet the requested deadline.

The Planned and Estimated Deadline

In this case the project manager and the project team, through their initial project management estimating process, determined the project completion date. There will be cases where, as a result of your initial planning (see Chapter Three), you will have the luxury of negotiating the completion date with the authorizing manager. "Guesstimating" a completion date often occurs as an initial step just to get the planning moving. However, estimating the project completion date requires time and a sound planning process. This date is obtained after the initial planning cycle of the project is completed.

Let us turn next to some concrete examples of the general discussion we have just presented. Remember, we are still preparing the project overview.

IDENTIFY PROJECT GOALS

Every project has only one major goal to be accomplished and several objectives that support that goal. The goal is the global statement of purpose and direction toward which all objectives, work activities, and tasks will point. The goal serves the following functions:

- It defines the final outcome in terms of the end product or services.

- It is the continual point of reference for settling disputes and misunderstandings about the project.

- It is the guide that keeps all objectives and the work associated with them on track.

The goal statement should be action-oriented, short, simple, straightforward, and as understandable as possible. Some examples will help clarify:

- Prepare and launch the space shuttle *Atlantis* on March 5, 2025, from Cape Canaveral, Florida.

- Connect France with England via a covered tunnel and paved roadway running under the English Channel and have that facility open for traffic no later than August, 1993.

- Design and complete pilot testing by September, 1994, a software package that performs basic financial analyses for small businesses.

- Obtain an MBA in management from Bentley College by spring, 2000.

Note that each of these goal statements tells precisely what will be done and by when. The end point may have to be revised after further review, but at this point the end date shows finality to the project.

LIST THE OBJECTIVES

In order to accomplish the stated goal, several major project steps will have to take place. These are the objectives, and they represent major components of the project (some would use the term *milestones*, which is perfectly acceptable). Objectives are not actual work that is accomplished but subgoals which direct work activity. They are more precise statements than the goal statement and, like goal statements, are also action-oriented. In order for the goal to be achieved, all objectives must be realized. George Doran (1981) has offered a meaningful and easy-to-remember guide for helping us formulate objective statements. His method is called S.M.A.R.T.

S pecific	Be specific in targeting an objective.
M easurable	Establish a measurable indicator(s) of progress.
A ssignable	Make the objective capable of being assigned to someone for completion.
R ealistic	State what can realistically be achieved within budgeted time and resources.
T ime-related	State when the objective can be achieved, that is, the duration.

For example, you may state as an objective, "Get a degree by next year." If you used the S.M.A.R.T. method, however, how would you revise this objective? First, you may ask, what kind of degree? Then, how realistic is it for me to obtain this degree? How much would it cost? When exactly would I graduate? After this analysis, you might revise your objective as follows: "Obtain a bachelor of arts, B.A., degree in clinical psychology at the University of Wisconsin, Madison, at the end of the spring semester, 1999." Think of an objective you wish to accomplish. Write it down, then apply the S.M.A.R.T. method. This requires practice and discipline. Writing S.M.A.R.T. objectives is essential for effective project planning.

By specifying objectives we begin to view the project in terms of its major components. Objectives are a crude roadmap that helps decision makers and other members of the management team to understand the scope of the project. They also provide a basis for determining resource requirements and the project timeline. At the end of the chapter we will give an example of goal and objectives statements which should clarify any confusion between the two.

WHAT CRITERIA WILL BE USED TO EVALUATE PROJECT SUCCESS?

It goes without saying that you are expected to complete the project on time, within budget, and according to specification. Specifications may include criteria, measures of success, as the following examples illustrate:

- At least 245 of the 280 delegates will register and attend the annual conference.

- The new product introduction will generate sales of $350,000 in the first six months.

- The new order entry system will be considered successful if the average time from order entry to order fulfillment is less than five working days; the average order value exceeds $1,000; less than 2 percent of orders are backordered; and there is less than one customer complaint per $100,000 ordered.

At this early stage of project preparation, a planning committee or task force can touch base with those individuals and groups who will be involved in the project in order to gather a preliminary list of success criteria against which the project outcomes can be measured. These criteria will most likely be revised as the project plan progresses.

DETERMINE PRELIMINARY RESOURCES

Don't think of resources only as money. Resources include human resources and materials as well as financial capital. Included on your list of resources will be people (how many, who, when, and for how long), equipment (what pieces, when, and for how long), and office space (for larger projects office space for you, an assistant project manager, and other support staff may be required). There are two scenarios to consider:

1. The resources were determined without project manager input

2. The project manager determined the needed resources based on the project plan

First Scenario

Like the predetermined "water cooler" imposed project deadline, resources may be allocated beforehand. Still, you will have to complete your planning before you know how adequate the resources given to you will be. Based on existing contracts and agreements with customers, you may have little choice, regardless of the adequacy of the resources given to the project. Patronizing management by agreeing to a level of support that you believe inadequate should be avoided. Similarly, requests for exotic support beyond that which has been identified by management is foolhardy. Prudence and common sense must prevail at this early, arbitrary stage. However, once your formal planning process is completed, you will have adequate documentation to argue for the necessary resources to complete each work assignment.

Second Scenario

You may be asked to present a preliminary plan in which you "guesstimate" needed resources. This scenario is preferable to being told what you have in order to complete a project. By following the steps offered in Chapter Three, you will be able to prepare the project resource requirements and then negotiate with the authorizing manager.

IDENTIFY ASSUMPTIONS AND RISKS

The project idea must often be sold to "higher ups" as well as to staff and review groups. Therefore, the project overview must be a persuasive statement. Don't forget: to effectively sell an idea, product, or service, you must believe in it and have confidence in its worth. At the same time it must be realistic. Identifying assumptions and risks associated with each objective is a step toward acknowledging your understanding of the assumptions and risks involved with the planning and completion of the project. Identifying the assumptions and risks also helps you think through the issues associated with executing the project. A guide to stating assumptions and risks is to take each objective you listed and ask the following questions:

1. What resources are required to realistically complete this objective? What risks are associated with obtaining any of these resources in a timely manner?

2. What problems and delays are likely to occur in completing this objective?

3. What effect(s) will delays have on the budget and overall project schedule and plan?

4. What are the probable time, money, and personnel cost overruns to complete this project?

5. What assumptions can be made to realistically correct for delays in completing this objective within given resources and constraints?

Once your project overview statement is done, complete the Quality Control Checklist and Acid Test at the end of the chapter. Then ask some trusted, competent colleagues to read, critique, and comment on the overview's "acceptance probability." Inform your colleagues of your intended audience, the people who must approve the idea.

The following example provides you with concrete information used to complete a project overview. Think through your own project ideas as you read.

EXAMPLE: PLANNING A PROFESSIONAL CONFERENCE

THE BIRTH OF A CONFERENCE

At the winter meeting of the Executive Council of the Program of Project Managers (PPM) it was decided that the organization's annual conference would take place in the early fall. As in the prior year, a staff of four and an operating budget of $50,000 (the same as last year) has been allocated to the project. Last year's conference was a disappointment in that the number of attendees had dropped for the third consecutive year and the conference barely broke even. Knowing that the bleeding had to stop, the goal for this year's conference was set at a net profit of $25,000.

There was some discussion over the choice of conference chairperson. On previous occasions you had expressed an interest in moving up to an officer position in PPM. Brad Kennedy, the Executive Director, knew of your interest. Because of your organizational and management skills, he saw a clear hero strategy for you if you could pull off a successful conference. He offered your name. Since no others were suggested, you got the job. You received the news with some trepidation, but being a risk taker you agreed to the assignment. It is fair to say that you weren't as convinced of the hero strategy as Brad. You felt that the downside risks weren't that great and it was your opportunity to make a play for that officer position.

Figure 2-1 is the project overview for the PPM Conference Planning Project. The first step to planning the conference project is to get the idea on paper. Therefore, we complete the project overview. The problem/opportunity statement is merely a reflection of the state of affairs in the PPM. The survival of the PPM depends on solving this problem of declining membership and conference attendance—the goal statement. More specifically, we can identify three separate objec-

Figure 2-1   PROJECT OVERVIEW REPORT FOR THE PPM ANNUAL CONFERENCE

PROJECT OVERVIEW	Project Name PPM Annual Conference	Project Manager

Problem/Opportunity

Membership in the Program of Project Managers (PPM) has dropped for the last four years and attendance at the annual conference has dropped for the last three years. The viability and financial stability of the organization depends heavily on our ability to maintain membership and conduct a successful annual conference.

Goal

Reverse the downward trend in membership and annual conference attendance.

Objectives

1. Conduct the PPM Annual Conference at an attendance level above that of three years ago.

2. Realize a net profit of at least $25,000 from the PPM Annual Conference.

3. Offer three concurrent tracks in the professional program, highlighting nationally known project management experts, that will draw both members and nonmembers to the PPM Annual Conference.

Success Criteria

1. At least 245 of the 280 delegates will attend.

2. At least 4% of the 23,000 members will attend.

3. At least 1.5% of the nonmembers receiving the conference brochure will attend.

4. At least 5% of the nonmember attendees will join PPM.

Assumptions

1. Interest in PPM can be renewed through the annual conference.

2. A quality professional program will attract members and nonmembers.

Prepared by	Date	Approved by	Date

tives that pertain directly to the annual conference and indirectly to the problem/opportunity statement. As an aside, note that there could be several other objectives that relate to the problem and that would have nothing to do with the annual conference. We could envision projects having to do with membership campaigns or image changes. Four measures of project success have been identified. Note that they relate directly to the problem/opportunity statement, too. Finally, there are two assumptions that have been made. These assumptions happen to be critical to the problem resolution, for without the causal linkage between a quality conference and membership, the project would not address the problem.

SUMMARY

At this point in the 5-phase project management process you should be able to

1. define a project;

2. list a project's characteristics;

3. distinguish a project from a task, an assignment, and a program;

4. state the first step in developing a project (the project overview);

5. state the basic parts of a project overview;

6. state the functions a project overview serves; and

7. write a saleable project overview for your project idea.

In the next two sections of this chapter you will find a project overview Quality Control Checklist and Acid Test. Use these lists to review your project overview and assign it a "go" or "no-go" status.

PROJECT OVERVIEW QUALITY CONTROL CHECKLIST

YES OR NO

1. Opportunity/Problem Statement

   _____ The need, problem, and/or opportunity has been stated clearly and realistically.

   _____ It is evident who experiences the need.

   _____ The effects of the project results are evident.

   _____ The benefit/gain is evident from reading the opportunity/problem statement.

2. Project Goal

____ The desired end result of the project has been clearly stated in the goal.

____ The goal statement is specific, measurable, time-related, and provides direction.

____ The goal can realistically be accomplished.

____ The goal is manageable.

3. Project Objectives

____ All objectives are complete and necessary to achieve the stated goal.

____ All objectives are stated clearly, simply, and realistically.

____ All objectives have a definable and measurable end result to be accomplished.

____ All objectives are finite, i.e., they each have a beginning and an end.

____ **S.M.A.R.T.** (specific, measurable, assignable, realistic, time-related).

4. Stated Risks, Assumptions, Questions

____ All risks, assumptions, and questions regarding the project have been stated at this point.

____ All risks, assumptions, and questions regarding the project are realistic and demonstrate knowledge of the activities to be completed.

____ The stated risks, assumptions, and questions enable reviewers of the project to assess benefits and costs in planning, implementing, and managing the project.

PROJECT OVERVIEW ACID TEST

1. The Project Overview as stated is understandable to an outsider.

2. The Project Overview as stated can be used to "sell" the project "up" and to others who would do the work.

3. The Project Overview as stated can be used to develop an action plan.

4. You would plan, implement, and manage the project overview as stated.

5. Your core project team reviewed and approved your project overview.

5-PHASE PROJECT MANAGEMENT

|←——— PLANNING ———→|←———————— IMPLEMENTATION ————————→|

1	2	3	4	5
DEFINE	**PLAN**	**ORGANIZE**	**CONTROL**	**CLOSE**
State the Problem	*Identify Project Activities*	Determine Personnel Needs	Define Management Style	Obtain Client Acceptance
Identify Project Goals	*Estimate Time and Cost*	Recruit Project Manager	Establish Control Tools	Install Deliverables
List the Objectives	Sequence Project Activities	Recruit Project Team	Prepare Status Reports	Document the Project
Determine Preliminary Resources	Identify Critical Activities	Organize Project Team	Review Project Schedule	Issue the Final Report
Identify Assumptions and Risks	Write Project Proposal	Assign Work Packages	Issue Change Orders	Conduct Post-Implementation Audit

|←———————————————— DELIVERABLES ————————————————→|

• Project Overview	• **WBS** • Project Network • Critical Path • Project Proposal	• Recruitment Criteria • Work Package Description • Work Package Assignments	• Variance Reports • Status Reports • Staff Allocation Reports	• Final Report • Audit Report

Chapter 3

SPECIFYING THE PROJECT

You have just completed a project overview. You reviewed and revised it with other professionals and/or experts, and then successfully sold it to "higher ups" in the organization—or to a bank, your boss, or yourself. You have confidence in the idea and you know your idea is a project. What's the next step?

In this chapter we present a simple decomposition process called a *work breakdown structure* (WBS). The WBS is a hierarchical representation of the project. It shows you how to identify the activities that must be done to begin and complete the project. At this point you have a goal and several objectives that must be expressed in terms of activities and work to be done. Our technique for generating the WBS will reduce even the most complex projects to activities and tasks that can be planned and executed with confidence. Later you will see that the WBS is the foundation for the more detailed definition, planning, organization, and control phases of the project management life cycle. It will be the document that guides the remainder of the project.

IDENTIFY PROJECT ACTIVITIES

To effectively plan and execute a complex project it is usually helpful to visualize the project as having an overall goal with several objectives. Each objective will have a number of discrete, separately identifiable activities. These activities define the work that must be done in order to accomplish the objectives. They must be formulated and specified so that they can be easily measured and their completion easily verified. Activities are identified by considering each objective and asking, "What activities must be done in order to complete the project?"

Like goals and objectives, activities must also be S.M.A.R.T. For example, consider the activity, "Completion of the final draft of a report." This is not well-defined because *completion* is a term subject to wide interpretation. A more specific activity statement would be, "Acceptance of the final draft." There is no doubt when this activity is to be finished. "Completion of the final draft" leaves one open to private interpretation of the expected final product. In other words, there can easily be disagreement over what is expected of the final draft.

21

"Approval," on the other hand, is not subject to interpretation—you either have it or you don't.

WORK BREAKDOWN STRUCTURES (WBS)

Of all the methods available to define the activities that comprise a project, the one that we have used extensively and that has withstood the test of time is the WBS. The concept of the WBS is easily understood and quickly mastered. It involves envisioning the project as a hierarchy of goal, objectives, activities, subactivities, and work packages. The hierarchical decomposition of activities continues until the entire project is displayed as a network of separately identified and nonoverlapping activities. Each activity will be single-purposed, of a specific time duration, and manageable; its time and cost estimates easily derived, deliverables clearly understood, and responsibility for its completion clearly assigned. Ideally, the final defined activities will be known entities. They have been done before or they are sufficiently similar to other known activities. As we will see, the WBS facilitates the planning, budgeting, scheduling, and control activities for the project manager and team.

CHARACTERISTICS OF A SUCCESSFUL WORK BREAKDOWN STRUCTURE

The first question to ask is, "How do I know that I have identified all the necessary activities to successfully achieve the project objectives?" First, let us look at the characteristics of the activities that comprise the WBS. A well-defined activity has the following characteristics:

- Its status and completion is easily measured.
- It has a very definite beginning and ending event.
- It is familiar (may have been done before) and the time to complete it and its associated costs can easily be estimated from prior experiences with this or similar activities.
- It comprises work assignments that are manageable, measurable, integrable, and independent of work assignments in other activities.
- It should normally constitute one continuous stream of work from start to finish.

In deciding on other activities that might be included in the project, consider the following:

- scheduling material delivery,

- subcontractor activities that impact project activities,

- equipment availability, and

- staff training and availability.

If these can affect project activities and hence project completion time, include them as activities in the WBS.

STEPS FOR CONSTRUCTING A WORK BREAKDOWN STRUCTURE

There are no specific rules that govern the creation of the WBS. However, a process that we have used successfully utilizes the form given in Figure 3-1. The following steps lead to completing the WBS:

Step 1:   Divide the project into its major objectives such that the project is fully defined by the objectives.

Step 2:   Partition each objective into the activities that must be done in order to accomplish the objective.

Step 3:   For each activity having one or more missing characteristics divide that activity into the subactivities comprising it.

Step 4:   Repeat step 3 until all subactivities have the characteristics desired.

Step 5:   The lowest-level subactivities in the hierarchy will be the basis of the work packages that must be done in order to complete the project.

Figure 3-2 is an example of the 5-step process for building a WBS. Figure 3-3 shows the corresponding WBS. Note the numbering system. The first digit identifies the project, the second identifies the activities that comprise the project, the third identifies subactivities within an activity, etc. This provides an easy reference according to the project hierarchy and facilitates computer input.

WORK BREAKDOWN STRUCTURE—HIERARCHICAL REPRESENTATION

A convenient graphical representation of the WBS is shown in Figure 3-4. For purposes of presentation, training, and project understanding, the graphical display is often preferred. It can be generated directly from the activity list on the WBS worksheet (see Figure 3-3).

Figure 3-1   WORK BREAKDOWN STRUCTURE—DEFINITION WORKSHEET

WBS WORKSHEET	Project Name	Project Manager
Activity No	Activity Description	Characteristics 1 2 3 4

Prepared by	Date	Activity Characteristics Legend
		1 Status/completion measurable.
Approved by	Date	2 Clearly defined start/end events. 3 Time/cost easily estimated. 4 Assignments manageable, measurable, integrable, and independent.
Sheet ____ of ____		

Figure 3-2   THE 5-STEP PROCEDURE FOR GENERATING THE WBS

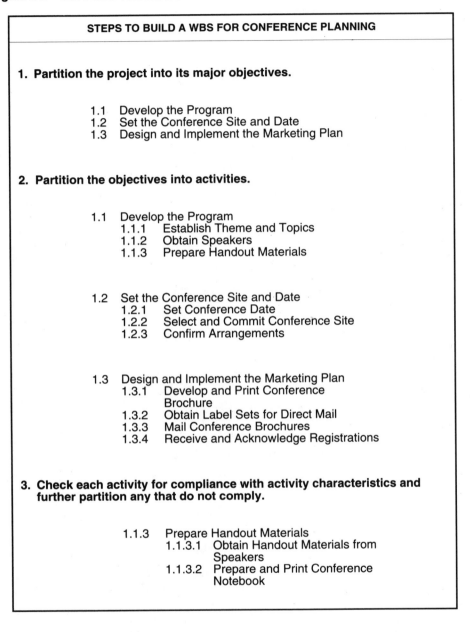

STEPS TO BUILD A WBS FOR CONFERENCE PLANNING

1. Partition the project into its major objectives.

    1.1 Develop the Program
    1.2 Set the Conference Site and Date
    1.3 Design and Implement the Marketing Plan

2. Partition the objectives into activities.

    1.1 Develop the Program
        1.1.1 Establish Theme and Topics
        1.1.2 Obtain Speakers
        1.1.3 Prepare Handout Materials

    1.2 Set the Conference Site and Date
        1.2.1 Set Conference Date
        1.2.2 Select and Commit Conference Site
        1.2.3 Confirm Arrangements

    1.3 Design and Implement the Marketing Plan
        1.3.1 Develop and Print Conference Brochure
        1.3.2 Obtain Label Sets for Direct Mail
        1.3.3 Mail Conference Brochures
        1.3.4 Receive and Acknowledge Registrations

3. Check each activity for compliance with activity characteristics and further partition any that do not comply.

        1.1.3 Prepare Handout Materials
           1.1.3.1 Obtain Handout Materials from Speakers
           1.1.3.2 Prepare and Print Conference Notebook

Figure 3-3   WBS WORKSHEET—PPM CONFERENCE PLANNING PROJECT

WBS WORKSHEET	Project Name PPM Annual Conference		Project Manager			
Activity No	**Activity Description**		**Characteristics**			
			1	**2**	**3**	**4**
1.1	Develop Program		Y	N	N	N
1.2	Set Conference Date		Y	Y	Y	N
1.3	Design and Implement Marketing Plan		Y	N	N	N
1.1.1	Establish Theme and Topics		Y	Y	Y	Y
1.1.2	Obtain Speakers		Y	Y	Y	Y
1.1.3	Prepare Handout Materials		Y	Y	Y	N
1.1.3.1	Obtain Handout Materials from Speakers		Y	Y	Y	Y
1.1.3.2	Prepare and Print Conference Notebook		Y	Y	Y	Y
1.2.1	Set Conference Date		Y	Y	Y	Y
1.2.2	Select and Commit Conference Site/Date		Y	Y	Y	Y
1.2.3	Confirm Arrangements		Y	Y	Y	Y
1.3.1	Develop and Print Conference Brochure		Y	Y	Y	Y
1.3.2	Obtain Label Sets for Direct Mail		Y	Y	Y	Y
1.3.3	Mail Conference Brochures		Y	Y	Y	Y
1.3.4	Receive and Acknowledge Registrations		Y	Y	Y	Y

Prepared by	Date	Activity Characteristics Legend
		1 Status/completion measurable. **2 Clearly defined start/end events.**
Approved by	**Date**	**3 Time/cost easily estimated.** **4 Assignments manageable,**
Sheet 1 of 1		**measurable, integrable,** **and independent.**

Figure 3-4   HIERARCHICAL REPRESENTATION OF THE CONFERENCE PLANNING WBS

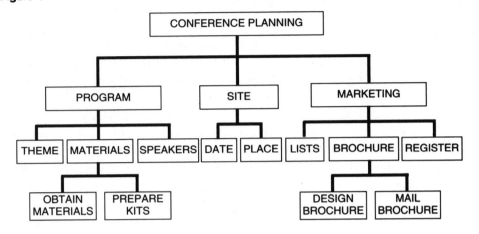

Uses of the Work Breakdown Structure

Just as the project overview was valuable during early planning activities, the WBS is valuable during the more detailed planning activities and early implementation. One of its major uses is to provide a global—yet detailed—view of the project. In this way, it will be the foundation for time, cost, and performance planning, and for control and reporting. As planning proceeds, the WBS will be used to generate a network representation (discussed in Chapter Four) of the project. This network will be the major control tool used by the project manager to evaluate planned versus actual progress and to manage the changes that will follow as a result of that evaluation.

The WBS is the easiest to learn and least error-prone technique we have encountered for representing the many tasks that comprise even the simplest of projects. It is a graphical representation that is easily understood by those having little familiarity with the details of the project. It is a tool that we will use in Chapter Four to build the network of project activities. The WBS therefore serves as an intermediate planning device.

There will be projects for which a network representation of a WBS may seem too difficult to generate. In those cases we have found it helpful to consider other approaches to defining the WBS. For example, the project may be decomposed by functional business unit, by geographic location, by department, according to the skills needed, or based on equipment or material availability. These alternatives may work in cases where the more straightforward hierarchical approach fails. The best advice we can give is to think creatively when developing the WBS.

ESTIMATE TIME AND COST

Now that the WBS is complete the next step will be to estimate the time and cost of each of the activities that comprise the project. Since each activity has the four characteristics listed in Figure 3-1, they will be sufficiently familiar (either having been done before or being similar to previous activities) that estimating time and cost will be straightforward. Let experience be your guide.

On the other hand, the project may be different from others your unit may have encountered. Even if the project is similar, there may be one or more activities that are new. In the next section we provide a simple technique for estimating activity time. And in the following section we will discuss a process for estimating activity cost.

ESTIMATING ACTIVITY TIME—HIGHLY SPECULATIVE SITUATIONS

The time to complete an activity is random. That is, if a given activity were done over and over again one would expect the completion times to vary somewhat. This will be true for even the most routine of activities. For some activities the observed completion times may vary considerably. For others they will be relatively stable. Reasons for these variations include:

- skill levels of the people doing the activity,

- machine variations,

- material availability, and

- unexpected events (sickness, natural disasters, worker strikes, industrial accidents, employee turnover, etc.).

We know these events will happen, but we cannot predict their occurrence on a specific project or activity with any accuracy. In some way, however, we are compelled to account for them. There is a statistical relationship that accounts for these variations quite well and is very easy to use. It requires only that we obtain three estimates of activity completion time:

1. Optimistic completion time

2. Pessimistic completion time

3. Most likely completion time

These estimates will often come from interviewing those whose experiences and expertise are valued, at least in relation to the activity at hand. The *optimistic completion time* of an activity is the time that will be required if everything goes perfectly. That is, if everything happens exactly when it should and there are no unexpected events that delay activity completion. The *pessimistic completion time* of an activity is the time required if everything that can go wrong does go wrong (Murphy's Law) but the activity is still completed. The *most likely completion time* of an activity is the time required under more normal situations. This may also be an estimate of the completion time that has occurred most frequently from prior experience with similar activities. In many cases all three of these times may be estimated from prior experiences with similar activities. The bottom line is to get as much information as you can regarding these times and let experience and good judgment be your guide.

To facilitate computation, let "O" represent the optimistic time, "P" represent the pessimistic time, and "M" represent the most likely time. We will use these three estimates to compute "E," the expected completion time of the activity. Therefore, for each activity we will need to get these three estimates.

Later in our computations we will need to use the average activity completion time. For reasons that are beyond the scope of this book, this is a weighted average of the optimistic, pessimistic, and most likely completion times. The following formula gives that weighted average:

$$\text{average activity completion time} = E = (O + 4M + P)/6$$

Figure 3-5 shows these calculations for the Conference Planning Project. In those cases where the activity time is fairly well known it is not necessary to obtain optimistic, pessimistic, and most likely activity completion times. Having a single estimated activity time is sufficient.

ESTIMATING ACTIVITY COST

There are typically four major cost categories (although the organization's chart of accounts might also be used) that may be defined for any activity:

1. Labor

2. Materials

3. Other direct (travel, telephone, contracted services, etc.)

4. Indirect (a.k.a. overhead)

In some cases indirect cost may be a fixed percentage of total direct costs attributable at the project level rather than at the activity level. As a general practice the

Figure 3-5 **ESTIMATED ACTIVITY TIMES FOR CONFERENCE PLANNING**

ACTIVITY		TIME (IN WEEKS)			
		(O)	(M)	(P)	(E)
A	Set conference date	1.0	2.0	3.0	2.0
B	Establish theme & program	2.0	5.0	8.0	5.0
C	Select conference site	4.0	5.0	6.0	5.0
D	Obtain speakers	4.0	6.0	8.0	6.0
E	Develop brochure	3.0	10.0	11.0	9.0
F	Obtain mailing labels	3.0	4.5	9.0	5.0
G	Mail brochure	1.0	2.0	3.0	2.0
H	Obtain speaker materials	3.0	3.5	7.0	4.0
I	Receive registrations	4.0	6.0	8.0	6.0
J	Confirm arrangements	0.5	1.0	1.5	1.0
K	Prepare conference kits	1.0	2.0	3.0	2.0

unallocatable costs, such as administrative overhead, utilities, building deprecia-
tion, etc., are computed as a fixed percentage of total direct costs. The reason for
this is that whenever changes occur at lower levels in the project, recalculation of
indirect costs will have to be made. A good rule to follow is to accrue indirect costs
at the highest level that makes sense. This may or may not be at the project level.
For large projects it generally will be at some lower level. Common sense is usually
the best judge here.

In the next two sections of this chapter you will find a WBS Quality Control
Checklist and Acid Test. Use these lists to assess whether all the necessary activities
needed to successfully achieve the project objectives have been identified.

PROJECT SPECIFICATION QUALITY CONTROL CHECKLIST

YES OR NO

_____ 1. All work activities under each objective have been identified.

_____ 2. Each activity will have a beginning and end time.

_____ 3. After the activities as stated are completed, the project goal will be accomplished effectively and efficiently.

_____ 4. The work activities are stated in a simple, clear, and realistic way. An
outsider could understand each one.

_____ 5. Each activity is discrete and does not temporally overlap any other.

_____ 6. The activities were identified by experts or experienced professionals.

_____ 7. Time, budgets, and personnel can be estimated for each activity's completion.

_____ 8. Each activity can be completed as described.

_____ 9. Each activity as stated can be managed.

_____ 10. One standard unit of time measurement was used for all activities.

_____ 11. A single time estimate was obtained for those activities whose estimated completion time is known.

_____ 12. Three estimates (optimistic, pessimistic, and most likely) were obtained for each speculative activity.

_____ 13. Appropriate documentation, including assumptions, risks, and other estimating procedures, is attached.

_____ 14. All costs for each activity have been estimated.

PROJECT SPECIFICATION ACID TEST

1. Each activity as stated is ready to be assigned and/or contracted out.

2. The benefits to the project each activity will provide are worth its costs.

3. You would assume responsibility for managing and holding others responsible for executing these activities.

4. Your core project team reviewed and approved your work breakdown structure.

5. You have used objective methods in estimating and activity time; your estimates are not biased by relying on persons you know to complete work.

6. Your activity time estimates are more conservative than risky.

7. You have documentation supporting the assumptions and decisions to go with these estimates.

8. You would put your job on the line to support your estimates.

9. Your core project team reviewed and approved your activity time estimates.

5-PHASE PROJECT MANAGEMENT

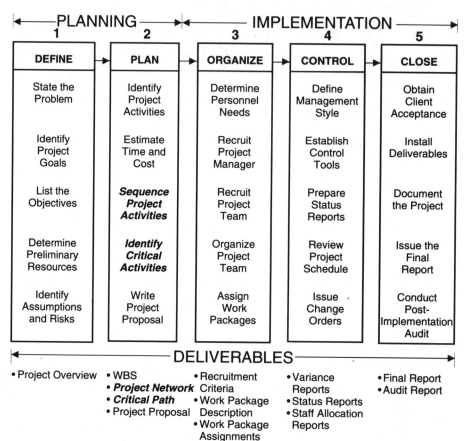

|◄————— PLANNING —————►|◄————————— IMPLEMENTATION —————————►|

1	**2**	**3**	**4**	**5**
DEFINE	**PLAN**	**ORGANIZE**	**CONTROL**	**CLOSE**
State the Problem	Identify Project Activities	Determine Personnel Needs	Define Management Style	Obtain Client Acceptance
Identify Project Goals	Estimate Time and Cost	Recruit Project Manager	Establish Control Tools	Install Deliverables
List the Objectives	*Sequence Project Activities*	Recruit Project Team	Prepare Status Reports	Document the Project
Determine Preliminary Resources	*Identify Critical Activities*	Organize Project Team	Review Project Schedule	Issue the Final Report
Identify Assumptions and Risks	Write Project Proposal	Assign Work Packages	Issue Change Orders	Conduct Post-Implementation Audit

|◄————————————————— DELIVERABLES —————————————————►|

• Project Overview	• WBS • ***Project Network*** • ***Critical Path*** • Project Proposal	• Recruitment Criteria • Work Package Description • Work Package Assignments	• Variance Reports • Status Reports • Staff Allocation Reports	• Final Report • Audit Report

Chapter 4

SEQUENCING THE PROJECT ACTIVITIES

The project is now represented as a list of activities. What is the next step? We must now determine the sequence in which these activities can be done. The simple approach would be to do them one at a time in some logical "to do" order. In all but the simplest of projects that approach would result in a project completion time much longer than one would have expected. Alternatively, one might examine each activity and determine which ones must be completed before others can begin. Through this analysis, a sequence in which several activities can be done simultaneously will emerge. In this chapter we present a simple step-by-step process, called the *critical path method* (CPM), to determine this sequencing of concurrent activities that results in the timely completion of the project. This critical path analysis provides the project manager with a tool to manage projects effectively and efficiently. The critical path method is explained on page 38.

SEQUENCE PROJECT ACTIVITIES

Using the activities as they are represented in the WBS we can construct the sequence in which the project activities will be done. Because each activity has an associated cost and an estimated completion time, we can build an estimate of the total project cost and completion time. Whereas the cost will basically be additive, the completion time will not. Simply recognizing that some activities may be done simultaneously and that others must be done sequentially is enough to grasp the complication in scheduling activities and estimating project completion time. For larger projects, of, say, 50 or more activities, a computer will be indispensable. Although we do not deal with this approach, the interested reader will have no difficulty locating sources for such computer programs. (See the Appendix for a discussion of project management software.)

A "low-tech" approach for the beginner at project management is to use Post-its® or gummed labels to lay out the network. Each label has one project activity written on it. Through an iterative process the labels can be arranged and rearranged until a realistic sequencing of project activities is obtained.

A powerful tool for estimating project completion time (it will have many other uses, too) is the representation of the project activities as a *network* of interconnected activities. The first step in building the network is to determine for each activity those activities that must be completed before this activity may begin. These are called *immediate predecessor* activities. Once this exercise is complete for all activities, the information necessary to construct the network will be assembled. The result of that exercise for the Conference Planning Project is shown in Figure 4-1. It is also a good idea to include the estimated completion times (E) for each activity, as we have done in Figure 4-1. We will add other information to this figure as we proceed with the process of constructing the network and analyzing the project activities.

Figure 4-1   ACTIVITY SEQUENCING FOR CONFERENCE PLANNING

ACTIVITY		IMMED PRED	TIME (IN WEEKS) (O)	(M)	(P)	(E)
A	Set conference date	-	1.0	2.0	3.0	2.0
B	Establish theme & program	-	2.0	5.0	8.0	5.0
C	Select conference site	A	4.0	5.0	6.0	5.0
D	Obtain speakers	B	4.0	6.0	8.0	6.0
E	Develop brochure	C,D	3.0	10.0	11.0	9.0
F	Obtain mailing labels	C,D	3.0	4.5	9.0	5.0
G	Mail brochure	E,F	1.0	2.0	3.0	2.0
H	Obtain speaker materials	D	3.0	3.5	7.0	4.0
I	Receive registrations	G	4.0	6.0	8.0	6.0
J	Confirm all arrangements	H,I	0.5	1.0	1.5	1.0
K	Prepare conference kits	J	1.0	2.0	3.0	2.0

PRECEDENCE DIAGRAMMING TECHNIQUES

We have now determined the "sequenced list" of project activities. What is the next step? The sequenced list contains all the information we need to proceed with the project, but does not represent it in a format that gives the "big picture." Our goal is to provide a graphical image of the project network, but in order to do that we need to instruct you in a few simple rules for drawing the project network.

Our basic "unit of analysis" in a sequenced network is the activity. Activities on the network will be represented by a rectangle which we call an "activity node," as shown in Figure 4-2. Don't worry about the symbols in the corners of the rectangle. They will be explained shortly. Every activity in the project will have its own activity node. The entries in the activity node describe the time-related properties of the activity. Some of the entries describe characteristics of the activity (Activity Number, for example), while others describe calculated values (ES, EF, LS, LF) associated with that activity. This format and terms are defined on page 37.

Figure 4-2   FORMAT OF AN ACTIVITY NODE

ES		EF
	Activity Number	E
LS		LF

The network will comprise these activity nodes and the connecting paths that describe the precedence relationships among the activities. The network diagrams are time-sequenced to be read from left to right. For example, Figure 4-3(a) shows that Activity A must be completed before Activity C can begin. Figure 4-3(b) shows that both Activities E and F must be complete before Activity G can begin. Finally, Figure 4-3(c) shows that Activities E and F may begin once Activities C and D are complete. Figure 4-3(c) also illustrates the situation where two activities (E and F) may be done simultaneously. Using these simple rules the network representation of the Conference Planning Project can be drawn. It is shown in Figure 4-4. Here are a few rules to follow in constructing the network:

1. Begin the network with a "start" node and end the network with an "end" node.

2. Sequence the nodes from left to right. That is, all the predecessor activities must appear in the network to the left of their successor activities.

3. There are no loops or backward flow sequences.

4. All nodes (except the start and end nodes) must have at least one predecessor and one successor node.

5. There are no "orphan" nodes; all nodes are connected.

6. A "path" is a sequence of all activities along each direction from the start to end nodes. Each network may have several paths.

Figure 4-3   EXAMPLES OF NETWORK GRAPHIC CONVENTIONS

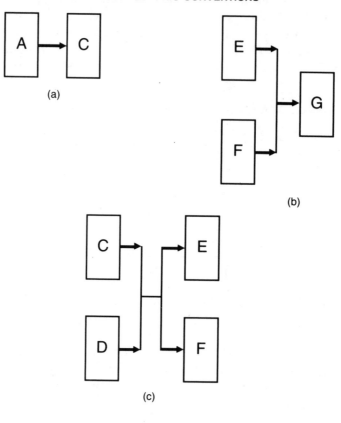

(a)

(b)

(c)

Figure 4-4   CONFERENCE PLANNING NETWORK

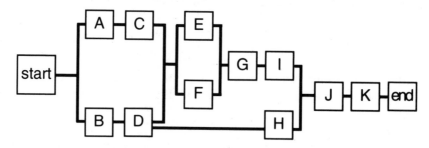

IDENTIFY CRITICAL ACTIVITIES

The most important use of the network is to determine the time required to complete the project and which project activities are critical to the project being completed on schedule. The time to complete the project is the longest time path through the network. The sequence of activities that makes up the longest path is known as the *critical path*. As long as activities on the critical path are going well, the project will remain on schedule. If, however, any of these activities takes longer than originally estimated, the project completion time will be extended. Of course, the manager will try to obtain additional resources for critical path activities to restore the project to its original completion date. Alternatively, when additional resources are available (say, from project activities that are not on the critical path), the manager may be able to reallocate them to critical path activities and get the project back on schedule.

ACTIVITY START AND COMPLETION TIMES

Now let us define the four calculated values (ES, LS, EF, LF, see Figure 4-2) associated with each activity node. These calculated values will be used to determine the project completion time and the critical path.

Earliest Start and Earliest Finish Times

The earliest start (ES) time for an activity is the earliest time at which all predecessor activities of that activity have been completed and the subject activity can begin. The ES time of an activity having no predecessor activities is arbitrarily set to 0. The EF time of an activity is equal to its ES time plus its estimated completion time. The ES time of an activity that has one predecessor activity is the EF time of the predecessor activity. The ES time of activities having two or more predecessor activities is the maximum of the EF times of the predecessor activities. The ES and EF times for the Conference Planning Project are shown in the upper left and right corners of each activity node (see Figure 4-5).

Latest Start and Latest Finish Times

The latest start (LS) and latest finish (LF) times of an activity are the latest times at which an activity can start (LS) or be completed (LF) without increasing project completion time. To calculate these times we will work backward in the network. First set the LF time of the last activity on the network to the EF time of that activity. The LS time of that activity is equal to its LF time minus its estimated completion time. The LF time of all the immediate predecessor activities is the minimum of the LS times of all activities for which it is the predecessor. The LS and LF times for the Conference Planning Project are shown in the lower left and right corners of each activity node (see Figure 4-5). The last numeric value in the node is the average

Figure 4-5 CONFERENCE PLANNING NETWORK SHOWING ES, LS, EF, AND LF TIMES FOR ALL ACTIVITIES

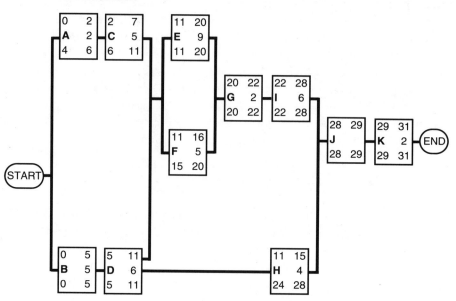

activity completion time (E) that is computed from the formula given in Chapter Three and repeated here:

$$E = (O + 4M + P)/6$$

LOCATING THE CRITICAL PATH

There are two ways to find the critical path in a network. The first way is simply to identify every possible sequence of activities through the network and compute the time to complete each of these paths. The sequence with the longest estimated completion time will be the critical path. This will work for smaller projects or for projects whose activities have mostly single predecessors. Figure 4-6 shows the calculation of all sequences of activities for the Conference Planning Project. Note that the sequence B–D–E–G–I–J–K, with a duration of 31 weeks, is the longest time path through the network and hence is the critical path.

For most projects this enumeration method is not feasible and we have to resort to the second method of finding the critical path. To do so we need to compute another quantity known as the activity slack time. *Slack time* is the amount of delay that could be tolerated in the starting time or completion time of an activity without causing a delay in the completion of the project. Slack time is mathematically the difference LS−ES (or equivalently, LF−EF). The sequence of activities having zero slack is defined as the critical path. Figure 4-7 highlights the critical path for the Conference Planning Project. Also in this figure, note the slack time placed above each activity node.

Figure 4-6 ALL POSSIBLE ACTIVITY SEQUENCES

PATH	DURATION
A - C - E - G - I - J - K	27 weeks
A - C - F - G - I - J - K	23 weeks
B - D - E - G - I - J - K	31 weeks <-- Critical Path
B - D - F - G - I - J - K	27 weeks
B - D - H - J - K	18 weeks

Figure 4-7 CRITICAL PATH AND SLACK TIME FOR THE CONFERENCE PLANNING NETWORK

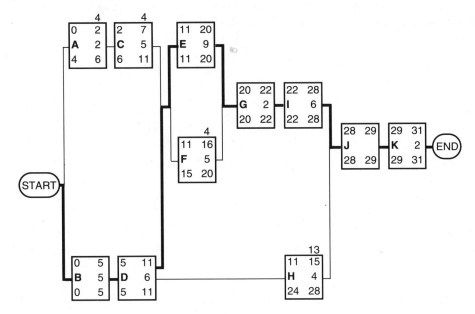

USE OF THE NETWORK AND CRITICAL PATH

The project network is a tool that the project manager and project team will use throughout the life of the project. For the project manager it is a tool for planning, implementation, and control. For the project team it is a tool to brief new team members on the project and its status.

Planning

Since the network shows the interdependencies between all project activities, it allows the manager to view the project in its entirety. This bird's-eye view of the project provides the manager with a tool for scheduling activity start times, assigning project team members to activities, and reallocating resources as the project commences. It is inevitable that the project will vary from the planned schedule, and you will need to move resources from activity to activity and make other adjustments to maintain the original completion date.

Implementation

As the project progresses, the network can be updated to reflect what has actually happened. Some activities will be completed in less time than originally estimated. This will give the project manager additional scheduling flexibility and the opportunity to reallocate resources to perhaps bring the project in earlier or for less cost. On the other hand, some activities will require more time to complete than was originally estimated. In these cases the project manager will first try to reallocate resources from non–critical path activities. If that doesn't provide enough additional resources, then a request for additional resources to get the project back on schedule will have to be made.

Control

By comparing the planned schedule of activities with what actually happened, the project manager will be aware of variances from plan and the appropriate corrective measures to take. In Chapter Nine we will examine this in more detail and provide additional reporting tools for analyzing and controlling project progress.

The Critical Path

The expected project duration time determined from the critical path analysis and the contracted project completion date provide useful pieces of information for making management decisions. For example:

• The scheduled start and completion date for each activity.

- The activities whose completion must occur exactly as scheduled in order for the project to be kept on schedule.

- The amount of delay that can be tolerated in non–critical path activities without causing a delay in the scheduled project completion date.

- Activities whose resources might be diverted to critical path activities if the need arises.

PROJECT NETWORK QUALITY CONTROL CHECKLIST

YES OR NO

_____ 1. The first node or activity is "start" at the left-hand side of the network; the last node is "end" at the far right-hand side.

_____ 2. The logic of sequencing activity nodes from left to right was done by asking, "What is the next activity that can begin only after the preceding activity is completed?"

_____ 3. "Time" was disregarded in this exercise; you are only concerned with which activity precedes and succeeds another activity.

_____ 4. No activity node should overlap any other. If so, make two discrete activities from that one.

_____ 5. All activity nodes flow from left to right in a linear way with no feedback loops.

_____ 6. All activity nodes are connected by a line on the network; no node is left unconnected.

_____ 7. All activities fit logically into the network; if not, the activity should be eliminated or re-created.

_____ 8. Each path can be easily traced from the start to the end node.

_____ 9. Parallel activity nodes on parallel paths can be drawn if work (activities) can be done simultaneously.

PROJECT NETWORK ACID TEST

1. An outsider could easily understand the sequencing of this project by studying your network diagram.

2. Each path can be traced with ease.

3. It is obvious which activities can be worked on simultaneously.

4. All activities are sequenced logically.

5. You are ready to pass this network up for approval.

6. Your core project team reviewed and approved the network.

5-PHASE PROJECT MANAGEMENT

← PLANNING →		← IMPLEMENTATION →		
1	**2**	**3**	**4**	**5**
DEFINE	**PLAN**	**ORGANIZE**	**CONTROL**	**CLOSE**
State the Problem	Identify Project Activities	Determine Personnel Needs	Define Management Style	Obtain Client Acceptance
Identify Project Goals	Estimate Time and Cost	Recruit Project Manager	Establish Control Tools	Install Deliverables
List the Objectives	Sequence Project Activities	Recruit Project Team	Prepare Status Reports	Document the Project
Determine Preliminary Resources	Identify Critical Activities	Organize Project Team	Review Project Schedule	Issue the Final Report
Identify Assumptions and Risks	***Write Project Proposal***	Assign Work Packages	Issue Change Orders	Conduct Post-Implementation Audit

← DELIVERABLES →

• Project Overview	• WBS • Project Network • Critical Path • ***Project Proposal***	• Recruitment Criteria • Work Package Description • Work Package Assignments	• Variance Reports • Status Reports • Staff Allocation Reports	• Final Report • Audit Report

Chapter 5

WRITING THE PROJECT PROPOSAL

The project proposal represents the transition from planning (define, plan) to implementation (organize, control, close). As we will see, it is the foundation on which the balance of the project rests and the basis on which all management decisions will be made.

In this chapter we examine the proposal in detail—paying particular attention to its component parts and their use as management tools.

PURPOSE

The purpose of the project proposal is to provide

- a statement of the need being addressed, the general approach being taken, and the resulting benefits expected;

- a complete description of the project activities, timeline, and resource requirements needed by management to decide whether the project should proceed to the implementation phase;

- a dynamic tool for the project manager and project team to use for decision making throughout the project life cycle;

- a reference document for management control;

- a briefing and training aid for new project team members; and

- a briefing document for others in the organization who need to be aware of the project details.

The proposal is clearly the key document in the project. It is simultaneously a tool for decision making, management control, training, and reporting. It is written to be understood and used by senior management, project management, project team members, other managers, and professionals with a need to know.

Let us first identify and describe each piece of information contained in the proposal. We will then illustrate with the proposal written for the PPM Conference Planning Project.

FORMAT

Figure 5-1 shows one format for the project proposal.

Project Name

This is a two- or three-word label that will uniquely identify the project. It becomes the name by which all will refer to the project.

Project Manager

The person responsible for the project. In some cases, especially projects to develop application software systems, the project manager may be the manager of the unit for which the project is being done. In any case, this is the person responsible for completing the project on time, within budget, and according to specification.

Activity

This is a three-part field that first identifies the activity by number (usually for computer input) and then by a short but descriptive name given to the activity. This is usually the way the project team and other interested parties will refer to the activity. Names such as XZ.40 are unacceptable. The preference will be to choose a name that is short but says something about the activity. "Schedule.Labels" is an example of a name we use in a later example. It gives some indication of the work to be done in this activity. The third part of the field is a description of the activity itself. It will be a specific statement in precise terms of the work to be done.

Schedule

Based on the analysis of the project network, the estimated start and end date of each activity is given. As the project progresses these dates may change. These are the dates on which the project manager will be ready to begin and expects to complete each activity in the project. All other dates given in the project (such as start and end dates for the tasks that comprise the work packages, discussed in Chapter Seven) are based on the assumption that the scheduled beginning date will be the actual beginning date.

Figure 5-1   PROJECT DEFINITION REPORT

PROJECT DEFINITION		Project Name							Project Manager				Date
Activity		Description	Schedule		Money	Budget						Manager	
			Start	End		Labor	Matls	Time (hrs)					
No	Name												
Prepared by		Date		Approved by			Date					Sheet ___ of ___	

Project Budget

The budget information on this report is aggregated at the activity level. More detailed information can be provided as attachments if that is the preference of top management. Budget planning is as much an art as it is a science. To see this, consider the following scenarios.

Underestimating Project Costs.   Management may balk at estimates of activity costs they perceive to be high, but there is no need to be overly optimistic nor pressured to the point of underestimating just to gain a favorable reaction. Senior management will often challenge an estimate, just to see if it is defensible.

It is not uncommon for less-experienced project managers to be too optimistic regarding both time and cost. In some cases such estimates may be given in order to be more competitive with other projects contending for management or customer support. In some cases estimates below cost may be given just to get the contract. Treating one project as a "loss leader" on the expectation that more projects will follow is not an unusual strategy.

Overestimating Project Costs.   Just as underestimating has its problems, so also does overestimating. Overestimating buys insurance against unexpected delays and problems that will require "going back to the well" and suffering the attendant embarrassment. The danger in overestimating, of course, is that management will not approve the project because the cost/benefit analyses suggest that approving the project would not be a good business decision.

Estimating the Budget.   The work breakdown structure, discussed in Chapter Three, provides the starting point for computing the project budget. Recall that the lowest-level activities in the WBS are the familiar activities. They, or similar activities, have been done before. Not only are activity time estimates available, but so are activity costs. Averaging techniques as well as inflation and other cost increases may have to be applied to get a current best estimate. As Figure 4-1 shows, resource needs are estimated at the intermediate level of the WBS. Backup detailed cost calculations can always be provided as attachments or appendices to the proposal. For the proposal itself, costs are estimated for each lowest-level activity and then aggregated following the hierarchy given by the WBS shown in Figure 3-4. Figure 5-2 is a typical format used in planning for the resource needs of a single project task. This may be given as an attachment to the Project Definition Report (Figure 5-1). Figure 5-3 shows the hierarchical breakdown of the entire Conference Planning Project budget.

Figure 5-2   WORK PACKAGE RESOURCE REQUIREMENTS REPORT

WORK PACKAGE BUDGET			Project Name		Project Manager		Date
			WP Name		WP Manager		Rev Date
Sch Start	Sch End	Critical Path Y/N	Predecessor Package No		Successor Package No		
Resource		Contact Person	Phone	Quantity	Sch Start	Sch End	
Prepared by		Date	Approved by		Date	Sheet ____ of ____	

Figure 5-3   ESTIMATED CONFERENCE PLANNING BUDGET

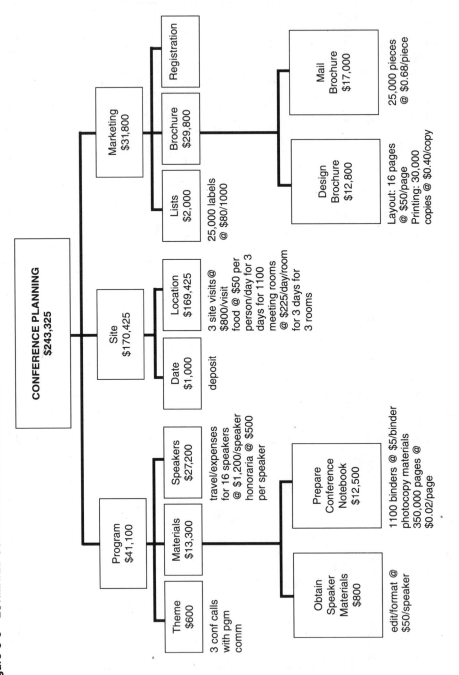

Revenue and Expense Estimates

Many projects will affect revenues. For example, the project may involve the planning, development, and distribution of new products/services; the repositioning of existing products/services, or the changes to any one of the steps in the logistics chain (procurement, manufacturing, inventorying, distribution); or problem resolution. These will all have financial implications, and senior management will want your best estimate of the impact on revenues and expenses before approval can be given. Figure 5-4 is a typical revenue and expense estimate for the Conference Planning Project.

PROJECT PROPOSAL QUALITY CONTROL CHECKLIST

YES OR NO

_____ 1. Experts and experienced people were used to help estimate and review each activity's budget.

_____ 2. All cost categories for each activity have been estimated (labor, equipment, travel, supplies, etc.).

_____ 3. Estimates for all internal resource costs were estimated before the need or use of external resources was estimated.

_____ 4. Cost estimates are realistic and conservative.

_____ 5. Cost estimates are comprehensive for each activity; there are no hidden costs or surprises.

PROJECT PROPOSAL ACID TEST

1. You have compared budgets across all activities and have determined any outstanding discrepancies.

2. The core project team has reviewed budget estimating methods and has approved consistency and objectivity.

3. Total project costs have been estimated and have your approval of reasonable need, no surprises, no hidden costs, no likelihood of cost overruns.

Figure 5-4   CONFERENCE PLANNING REVENUE AND EXPENSE BUDGET

PPM ANNUAL CONFERENCE REVENUE & EXPENSE BUDGET

Revenues
Registrations - 1100 @ $335 .... $368,500

Expenses
Salary
Graphic artist 800
Total Salary 800

Non-Salary
Travel 21,600
Printing 19,000
Postage 17,000
Mailing Lists 2,000
Telephone 600
Supplies 6,300
Speaker Honoraria 8,000
Site Deposit 1,000
Food 165,000
Meeting Room Rental 2,025
Total Non-Salary 242,525

Total Expenses $243,325

Gross Profit $125,175

Indirect (@ 40% of Total Expenses) $97,330

Net Profit $27,845

Part II

IMPLEMENTING THE PROJECT

Once the project is approved the real work begins. In terms of the project management life cycle, we have completed the planning phases and are moving into the implementation phases. Implementation begins with the formation of the project team and follows with the scheduling and assignment of work packages. As work progresses the project manager utilizes a system of reports and controls to keep the project on schedule and within budget. Implementation is complete when the project deliverables have been accepted by the client and made operational and all final reports have been filed. The details of the implementation phases are the topics of the next five chapters.

5-PHASE PROJECT MANAGEMENT

← PLANNING →		← IMPLEMENTATION →		
1	**2**	**3**	**4**	**5**
DEFINE	**PLAN**	**ORGANIZE**	**CONTROL**	**CLOSE**
State the Problem	Identify Project Activities	*Determine Personnel Needs*	Define Management Style	Obtain Client Acceptance
Identify Project Goals	Estimate Time and Cost	*Recruit Project Manager*	Establish Control Tools	Install Deliverables
List the Objectives	Sequence Project Activities	*Recruit Project Team*	Prepare Status Reports	Document the Project
Determine Preliminary Resources	Identify Critical Activities	*Organize Project Team*	Review Project Schedule	Issue the Final Report
Identify Assumptions and Risks	Write Project Proposal	Assign Work Packages	Issue Change Orders	Conduct Post-Implementation Audit

← DELIVERABLES →

• Project Overview	• WBS • Project Network • Critical Path • Project Proposal	• *Recruitment Criteria* • Work Package Description • Work Package Assignments	• Variance Reports • Status Reports • Staff Allocation Reports	• Final Report • Audit Report

Chapter 6

ORGANIZING THE PROJECT TEAM

Project plans and their execution are only as successful as the manager and team who implement them. Building effective teams is as much an art as it is a science. Some would in fact call it a craft. In building an effective team, consideration must be given not only to the technical skills of the project manager and the team members but also to their critical roles and the chemistry among them. The selection of project manager and team members will not be perfect—there is always a risk with any personnel decision. In this chapter we will

1. create an awareness of the important characteristics that should be part of an effective project manager and project team,

2. provide a checklist to assist you in your selection process, and

3. suggest guidelines for organizing the project in an organization.

DETERMINING PERSONNEL NEEDS: SELECTING THE PROJECT MANAGER

The project manager is one of the most important personnel in the project. This person plays a major role in planning and executing a project. The project manager also embodies the image and reality of the project to the organization and to external groups. Harold Kerzner (1982) states that because the roles and responsibilities of the project manager are so important, selection should be general management's responsibility. In large organizations a group or committee is usually assigned to help screen project manager candidates. This committee should

- use a set of selection criteria that includes final product/service specifications and profit objectives, in addition to professional qualifications;

- have a policy directive from corporate management for selecting a project manager; and

- involve and obtain the support of corporate management in the selection process.

If you are the project manager or are on the task force to hire one, this chapter can help you organize your thinking about the selection and organizing process for the project manager and the team before you get started.

TIMING

The timing in selecting a project manager varies. In larger organizations, the project manager can be assigned after the proposal giving the "go" to the project has been signed by senior management. One rule to remember is, "The sooner the project manager and team are involved in planning the project, the more committed they will be to its implementation." (This is also true for other members in the organization whose expertise and resources are required to implement the project.)

SELECTION CRITERIA

The major goal in selecting a project manager is: to assign someone who is experienced, capable, and competent in getting the end product or service planned and implemented on time, within budget, and according to specifications. Toward that end, the predominant characteristics of an effective project manager can be summarized under five categories:

1. Background and experience
2. Leadership and strategic expertise
3. Technical expertise
4. Interpersonal competence/people skills
5. Proven managerial ability

No single set of characteristics under any one category can be sufficient justification to hire a project manager. The categories presented here provide a balanced set of general characteristics for reviewing a candidate. The Project Manager Selection Quality Control Checklist at the end of the chapter provides a detailed review of these characteristics, which are summarized below.

Background and Experience

The background and expertise of a prospective project manager should be consistent with the nature and needs of the project requirements. As one saying goes, "A drop of experience can outweigh a ton of theory." Again, the goal is to assign someone who can get the job done within the means specified. The project manager should have a solid educational background in addition to experience in the desired project area. As a rule of thumb, you should look for a candidate who shows an acceptable mix of conceptual, analytical, operational, and practical experience.

Leadership and Strategic Expertise

The project manager is a leader who helps design, coordinate, control, and implement the project plan. The project leader stays the course until the project delivers the final product. Leadership and strategic expertise mean the ability to envision and actually design the "big picture," or all phases of project planning and implementation, while working on detail. It means seeing the forest in spite of the trees. Strategic expertise also involves the ability to ask guiding questions which direct the goal and planned end result through the critical path. A project manager should be able to separate strategic thinking, planning, and decisions from tactical or operational aspects of the project. Again, results-oriented experience and training of candidates are among the best indicators of strategic planning and implementation ability.

Technical Expertise

No project manager has all the technical expertise necessary to get a complex project completed. However, you are looking for a person who can direct, evaluate, and make sound decisions on technical alternatives related to the project. A project manager, then, should have technical expertise based on knowledge and training both in the content area of the project domain and in project management tools and skills. Kerzner (1982) states that technical skills—and here he focuses on engineering-related projects—include:

- Technology involved
- Engineering tools and techniques
- Specific markets, customers, and requirements
- Product applications

- Technological trends and evolutions
- Relationship among supporting technologies
- People who are part of the technical community

Whatever the nature of the project, project managers should have work experience in one of its significant areas, whether construction, technology hardware or software, educational training techniques, or conference planning. Project managers should understand the markets, customs, and technologies involved in the project and be associated with the networks of professionals in the technical field of their profession. The checklist provided below may seem at first glance too perfect or complete for anyone to actually qualify; remember, it is a guide.

Interpersonal Competence/People Skills

The project manager should be able to

- motivate, inspire, cheerlead, and coach;
- actively listen and give and receive meaningful feedback;
- assertively—not aggressively or submissively—relate feelings, needs, concerns, and interpersonal issues of the project to and among others;
- prevent as well as solve conflicts;
- communicate tough decisions yet be sensitive to others' needs; and
- be flexible—perform well in multiple roles.

Mintzberg (1973) identifies such traits as: figurehead, liaison, information disseminator, entrepreneur, negotiator, conflict resolver, and resource allocator. Other important roles include politician, salesperson, power broker, facilitator, monitor, and counselor. Indicators of interpersonal competence include favorable recommendations from past successful project personnel who worked with or under the candidate.

Proven Managerial Ability

The past is one of the best indicators of the future. Managerial ability is evident in a track record of getting the end product or service accomplished within budget, time, and resource constraints. To do this, a project manager should have a basic knowledge of organizations: how to organize, determine personnel needs, articulate project needs, interface with all levels of management, link the project goal to an enterprise mission, and reward and discipline employees.

Other rules of thumb in looking for effective management skills include screening individuals who can

- manage entrepreneurs,
- use organizational resources without being overly bureaucratic,
- relate effectively and comfortably upwardly, horizontally, and downwardly in large organizations, and
- give as well as take credit for tasks accomplished.

DETERMINING PERSONNEL NEEDS: SELECTING THE PROJECT TEAM

Once the project manager is on board, that person can help select the core project team members. Selecting the project team depends on a number of factors:

- The goal and objectives of the project
- The nature of the technical work to be done
- The expertise required to recruit, assign, delegate, monitor, communicate, and perform the required work in each phase of the project
- Availability of project personnel in the organization where the project will be housed

SELECTION CRITERIA

The same criteria used for selecting a project manager can be used for the team. Less emphasis can be placed on strategic leadership capability and more on technical specialization. Interpersonal competencies are important, and the same characteristics listed above can be used here, with less emphasis on leadership and figurehead functions.

As part of our project management consulting work we have compiled a list of project team member characteristics which high-technology engineers, in particular, have found to be successful. The following are borne out through experience with project teams, regardless of the nature of the project:

- Commitment to the project goal and its completion
- Ability to communicate and share responsibility and power

- Flexibility; able to shift from one work activity to another, depending on project schedule and need

- Technical competence

- Willingness to admit error and bias and be corrected

- Task-oriented

- Ability to understand and work within schedules and resource constraints; willing to work overtime if necessary

- Ability to trust, help others, and be helped

- A team player, not a self-oriented hero

- Entrepreneurial, but open to suggestions

- Ability to work with two or more bosses

- Ability to work without and across formal structure and authority systems

- Have knowledge and experience with project management tools

ORGANIZING AND HOUSING THE PROJECT

Now that the project manager and the project team are ready to go to work, how will they be organized, and where will they be located? There is no one best way to organize a project. Depending on the nature of the project, the resources needed and who needs to be communicating with whom and how often will determine the organizational form and position of the project in the larger organization. It is possible that your project will be independent of the larger organization, or that you are planning a project apart from an organization. If that is the case, the organizing question is less complicated.

Often, a "project office" (Kerzner, 1982) is organized and operated by the project manager. The project team is a combination of the office and the functional employees. The project office is a focal point for the project personnel to interact externally with customers and internally with different units of the organization.

If you must connect your project to a larger organization, Meredith and Mantel (1989) offer the following criteria for helping determine the organizational location:

- List the major desired project outcomes by objective.

- List the key tasks by objective and locate the functional organizational units for each task.

- Break the key tasks down into work packages.

- Determine which project subsystems are required to complete the work packages and which will work closely with others.

- List the special characteristics and assumptions of the project (technology, personnel, etc.).

- Choose a structure and location based on the above analysis.

With these guidelines in mind, the project manager can then assign team members to different functional areas in the organization, with the sign-off of those functional area managers. However, if the project manager decides to organize the project team with other organizational units, this must be done through the authority of general management. Remember, the goal is to get the project goal accomplished on time, within budget, and according to specifications. Organizing and housing the project are means to this end, not an end in itself.

There is no one easy, fixed way to organize a project team. Flexibility is the key, and working within and across organizational units is the norm. It is the project manager who in concert with the team develops both psychological and written contracts that assist the cross-functional roles and responsibilities.

PROJECT MANAGER SELECTION QUALITY CONTROL CHECKLIST

YES OR NO

The project manager

_____ 1. is experienced enough in this project area to successfully commit to complete the project on time, within budget, and according to specifications;

_____ 2. is strategically capable to envision and conceptualize the entire project process through all phases;

_____ 3. is technically competent to help design and execute a total project plan;

_____ 4. is interpersonally able and experienced to inspire, motivate, discipline, resolve conflicts, negotiate competing interests, and sell the project to corporate and other managers;

_____ 5. demonstrates the following competencies and characteristics: flexible, self-motivated, energetic, organized, alert, quick-to-learn, self-disciplined, effective listening skills, excellent problem solver, skilled politician, balanced temperament, sensitive, politically savvy, ethical, able to sell ideas and plans, express enthusiasm, cheerlead, coach, able to effectively interact verbally and nonverbally in the board room and on the shop floor, operates well under pressure;

_____ 6. demonstrates competency to act effectively and quickly in the following roles: figurehead, leader, liaison, monitor, information disseminator, spokesperson, entrepreneur, disturbance handler, resource allocator, negotiator; and

_____ 7. demonstrates effectiveness and experience in: understanding and interacting with customers and end users, meeting management, contract negotiations, all phases of strategic and technical planning, budgeting, resource acquisition and allocation, initiating and terminating professional and personal relationships, understanding complex organizational, group, and interpersonal issues and problems, admitting error and bias, acknowledging and celebrating others' contributions.

PROJECT TEAM SELECTION QUALITY CONTROL CHECKLIST

YES OR NO

The project team members

_____ 1. are committed to planning and executing the project through all phases;

_____ 2. are technically experienced in their specific area to help successfully complete the project on time, within budget, and according to specifications;

_____ 3. understand and have used project management concepts and tools;

_____ 4. are interpersonally capable of sharing information and expertise, solving conflicts jointly, planning and problem solving with others, actively listening, receiving and giving nonjudgmental feedback, communicating assertively;

_____ 5. are able to work with two or more bosses;

_____ 6. are self-motivated and entrepreneurial but not self-oriented;

_____ 7. are flexible;

_____ 8. are responsible and can own mistakes as well as achievements;

_____ 9. can share rewards and failures;

_____ 10. are willing to delegate and be delegated changing work assignments; and

_____ 11. can work well under pressure and changing deadlines.

PROJECT MANAGER AND TEAM SELECTION ACID TEST

The project management team is organized when

1. General corporate management issues policies, procedures, or directives for selecting/hiring the project manager and project team members.

2. General corporate management remains informed and directly active in the selection process.

3. General corporate management hires or selects the project manager and project team members and announces the assignments to the organization.

4. A project "home" is organized and positioned in relationship to the larger organization.

5. Corporate management announces and supports the organizational location and lines of authority of the project team.

6. The project manager and project team members begin work on the project.

5-PHASE PROJECT MANAGEMENT

PLANNING		IMPLEMENTATION		
1	2	3	4	5
DEFINE	**PLAN**	**ORGANIZE**	**CONTROL**	**CLOSE**
State the Problem	Identify Project Activities	Determine Personnel Needs	Define Management Style	Obtain Client Acceptance
Identify Project Goals	Estimate Time and Cost	Recruit Project Manager	Establish Control Tools	Install Deliverables
List the Objectives	Sequence Project Activities	Recruit Project Team	Prepare Status Reports	Document the Project
Determine Preliminary Resources	Identify Critical Activities	Organize Project Team	Review Project Schedule	Issue the Final Report
Identify Assumptions and Risks	Write Project Proposal	*Assign Work Packages*	Issue Change Orders	Conduct Post-Implementation Audit

DELIVERABLES

• Project Overview	• WBS • Project Network • Critical Path • Project Proposal	• Recruitment Criteria • *Work Package Description* • *Work Package Assignments*	• Variance Reports • Status Reports • Staff Allocation Reports	• Final Report • Audit Report

Chapter 7

ASSIGNING WORK PACKAGES

Planning and organizing are now complete and it's time to get down to the work of doing the project. The first step will be to assign responsibilities for completing the activities that comprise the project. Some of the activities will be familiar because they, or something very similar, have been done before. These will be rather straightforward and can be routinely assigned. For our purposes here they may be treated exactly like "work packages," the subject of this chapter. *Work packages*, the basic unit of work that takes place in the project, are like "contracts" between the project manager and the work package manager (or work package leader), the person charged with the responsibility of completing the tasks that comprise the work package.

First we define the work package. After examining its characteristics we discuss assigning responsibility for its completion on time, within budget, and according to specifications. Managing work packages is aided through the use of simple forms that define exactly what is to be done, by when, and by whom. The same form can be used to monitor the status of work packages. The form is simple in its use here but may be modified with more detail depending on the practices and procedures in your organization.

WHAT IS A WORK PACKAGE?

Recall that the WBS decomposed the project into a list of activities. Each activity contains specific tasks to be completed. These tasks may involve more than one individual, and, in a sense, for the individual assigned the responsibility of completing them, may be considered projects in their own right.

A work package consists of one continuous activity, for example, the use of a single piece of equipment, until the work package is complete. The work package is assigned to one individual who has the authority and access to the resources needed to complete the assignment. A successful work package will be clearly defined. It will have definite beginning and ending tasks so that its completion will

Figure 7-1   WORK PACKAGE DESCRIPTION REPORT

WORK PACKAGE DESCRIPTION			Project Name PPM Annual Conference		Project Manager You		Date
			WP Name Mailing		WP Manager Diane		Rev Date
Sch Start wk 11	Sch End wk 16	Critical Path Y/N no	Predecessor WP		C&D	Successor WP G	
		Task			Schedule		
No	Name		Description	Start	End	Responsibility	Phone
F.1	Target		Identify target markets for conference attendees			Diane	
F.2	Brokers		Locate appropriate list brokers to supply labels for each target market			Diane	
F.3	Target.Size		Determine size of each target market in the list broker's data base			Diane	
F.4	Build.Label.Set		Construct label set from each target market based on the expected yield and objective of 1100 attendees at the conf			Diane	
F.5	Schedule.Labels		Schedule the label set run for each list broker to coincide with the expected date the brochure will be available			Diane	
Prepared by			Date	Approved by		Date	Sheet ___ of ___

be easily measured and clearly observed. In Figure 7-1 we continue with our example of the Conference Planning Project. One of the most important parts of the work package, as indicated in Figure 7-1, is the description of each of the tasks that comprise it. Note that the descriptions of these tasks give a clear statement of the deliverables expected. Each task is considered complete (and hence the work package is considered complete) when the expected deliverable has been provided.

Work packages must be documented in other ways also. They are part of a network of interrelated work packages; therefore the project manager as well as the persons responsible for other work packages will have a need to know. Work package documentation must be standardized across the project and serve at least six purposes:

1. To inform all parties working on the activity, as well as on all predecessor and successor activities, of the contracted deliverables and expected completion dates

2. To record the project and be of value not only to the project manager but also to future project managers

3. To provide sufficient detail and description of all the tasks that comprise the work package and of the relationship of the work package to other work packages and to the project

4. To be presented in a format that can be updated and provide information for periodic project status reports

5. To hold the work package manager responsible for the successful completion of the tasks that comprise the work package

6. To serve as a reference point for clarifying issues and conflicts that may arise

SCHEDULING WORK PACKAGES

Scheduling the starting date for the work packages depends on the resource availability and the time constraints imposed by the project network. For any given project there will be a number of different resources required, such as manpower, facilities, and equipment. Each will have to be considered independently in scheduling the work packages that utilize them. To see just how this works, let us schedule the work activities for the Conference Planning Project around the available manpower resources. Our objective will be to level the use of manpower across the project by shifting activity start times within their allowable slack time. For the project manager, a balanced level of resource use across the project life cycle is preferred.

66   Assigning Work Packages

Figure 7-2   WORK PACKAGE ASSIGNMENT SHEET

WP ASSIGNMENT REPORT			Project Name PPM Annual Conference		Project Manager	
Activity						
No	Name	Description	Start	End	Manager	Phone
A	Select.Date	Identify dates that will not conflict with competing conferences or holidays	3/4	3/15	Andy	
B	Est.Theme	Recruit a committee to identify a theme, seminar topics, potential speakers	3/4	4/5	Beth	
C	Select.Site	Investigate availabilities of approved sites on the dates identified, solicit bids, and contract with chosen site	3/18	4/19	Andy	
D	Get.Speakers	Contact potential speakers, request their participation, and get signed commitment	4/8	5/17	Beth	
E	Dev.Brochure	Request bio and speech info for brochure. Submit to the graphic artist for design and approval. Print 30,000.	5/20	7/19	Carl	
Prepared by		**Date**	**Approved by**		**Date**	**Sheet 1 of 3**

Figure 7-3 PRELIMINARY WORK PACKAGE SCHEDULING AT EARLIEST START TIME

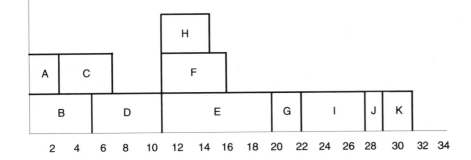

Figure 7-2 defines five work packages and assigns them to three staff members based on their expertise and past conference involvement. Figure 7-3 is a graphical representation of the workload on the project team when project activities are scheduled to begin at their earliest start date. It was constructed directly from Figure 4-7. Note that Activities E and F are scheduled to be done concurrently. That requires Carl to work concurrently on both activities. Activity F is not on the critical path and so its start date could be delayed. Unfortunately, Activity F does not have enough slack time to delay its start long enough for Carl to complete Activity E and then work on Activity F without delaying the project further. An alternative is to delay Activity H and have Beth work on Activity F. Figure 7-4 shows how the workload will be distributed with this change being made. The project manager will want to consider these scheduling alternatives for non–critical path activities in order to balance resource requirements across the entire project.

Figure 7-4 WORK PACKAGE SCHEDULING TO BALANCE THE WORKLOAD

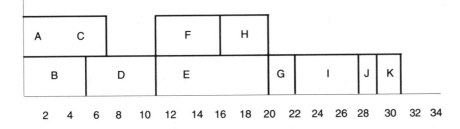

USING WORK PACKAGE ASSIGNMENTS FOR STAFF DEVELOPMENT

Motivating project team members is a continual problem for the project manager. One technique that we have used successfully is to match team members to tasks in such a fashion that some new skill must be learned by the team member in order to successfully complete the work package on schedule. Most professional people will rise to the challenge of something new—a motivation in itself. We are aware of the risks for the project manager, but suggest that in the long term there may be value in using the tasks as learning opportunities for career and skill development. Consideration should be given before forging ahead and making assignments based solely on the individual's mastery of the skills needed to complete a given assignment.

PROJECT WORK PACKAGE QUALITY CONTROL CHECKLIST

YES OR NO

_____ 1. The work package consists of tasks each of which are continuous activities that can be assigned to a single individual.

_____ 2. The deliverables expected from each task in the work package are clearly defined and measurable according to established standards and controls.

_____ 3. The work package documentation identifies all predecessor and successor work packages.

_____ 4. The work package report format can be easily updated and used as a status report, too.

_____ 5. The scheduled start and end date for every task in the work package has been specified.

_____ 6. The work package managers clearly understand what is expected and by when.

_____ 7. The resources necessary for each work package have been committed and are available according to the project schedule.

_____ 8. The task descriptions have been reviewed and approved by the work package manager and the project manager for completeness.

_____ 9. The persons responsible for the tasks that comprise the work package have reviewed and understand their task, the expected deliverables, and the timeline.

PROJECT WORK PACKAGE ACID TEST

1. The work package defines tasks whose completion will guarantee the successful accomplishment of the activity.

2. The work package managers have the necessary skills to accomplish their work.

3. The work package schedules are realistic.

5-PHASE PROJECT MANAGEMENT

PLANNING		IMPLEMENTATION		
1	**2**	**3**	**4**	**5**
DEFINE	**PLAN**	**ORGANIZE**	**CONTROL**	**CLOSE**
State the Problem	Identify Project Activities	Determine Personnel Needs	*Define Management Style*	Obtain Client Acceptance
Identify Project Goals	Estimate Time and Cost	Recruit Project Manager	Establish Control Tools	Install Deliverables
List the Objectives	Sequence Project Activities	Recruit Project Team	Prepare Status Reports	Document the Project
Determine Preliminary Resources	Identify Critical Activities	Organize Project Team	Review Project Schedule	Issue the Final Report
Identify Assumptions and Risks	Write Project Proposal	Assign Work Packages	Issue Change Orders	Conduct Post-Implementation Audit

DELIVERABLES

• Project Overview	• WBS • Project Network • Critical Path • Project Proposal	• Recruitment Criteria • Work Package Description • Work Package Assignments	• Variance Reports • Status Reports • Staff Allocation Reports	• Final Report • Audit Report

Chapter 8

MANAGING PEOPLE AND PROJECT RELATIONSHIPS

SEVEN HABITS OF HIGHLY EFFECTIVE PEOPLE

Effective management and control of project relationships involve

1. project leadership,

2. project "followership," and

3. motivating and relating effectively to others in the project and organization.

In this chapter we offer guidelines for managing individual and team relationships aimed at effectively increasing the progress of the project. It is true that the "plan and the tasks are the boss." It is also true that the project manager and the team must work well together and with other personnel involved in the project to accomplish the goal. Since project managers and teams must communicate with several bosses across organizational boundaries and turfs, interpersonal skills are a premium.

In his book *The 7 Habits of Highly Effective People* (1989), Stephen Covey lists seven habits which we offer as guiding principles for effective project leadership and "followership":

1. Be proactive.

2. Begin with the end in mind.

3. Put first things first.

4. Think win/win.

5. Seek first to understand, then to be understood.

6. Seek synergies (the whole is equal to *more* than the sum of its parts; so too the team adds more value than the number of its members).

7. Sharpen the saw (i.e., seek balance and self-renewal).

12 GUIDELINES FOR EFFECTIVE PROJECT LEADERSHIP

To manage a project effectively, a project manager must adopt a leadership style that both motivates and empowers team members and monitors and guides their progress. The following 12 guidelines from Raudsepp (1987) are offered as a resource for managing people in the project. These guidelines focus on flexibility.

1. Do not overdirect, overobserve, or over-report.

2. Recognize differences in individuals. Have a keen appreciation of each person's unique characteristics.

3. Help subordinates see problems as changes.

4. Assess your employees regarding ways they think they are more creative or would like to be most creative, and what sort of creative contribution they would most like to make.

5. Allow more freedom for individuals to guide their own work.

6. Train yourself and the others to respond to the positive parts of proposed ideas rather than react to the often easier-to-spot negative ones.

7. Develop greater frustration tolerances for mistakes and errors.

8. Provide a safe atmosphere for failures.

9. Be a resource person rather than a controller, a facilitator rather than a boss.

10. Act as a buffer between employees and outside problems or "higher up" demands.

11. Enhance your own creative ability through special workshops and seminars, specialized reading, and practice of creative exercises and games. This sets an excellent example employees will want to emulate, and makes it easier for you to recognize and relate to the creative ability of others.

12. Make sure that innovative ideas are transmitted to your boss with your support and backing; then insist on a feedback mechanism. Without feedback, the flow of creative ideas dries up because innovators feel that their ideas are not given a fair hearing or taken seriously.

MANAGING ACROSS FUNCTIONAL BOUNDARIES

Project managers and team members who manage projects within larger organizations must communicate, sell ideas, negotiate, problem solve, and resolve conflict across functional and sometimes geographic boundaries. Since the project leader and team are almost always "between" authority and control structures in the larger organizations, they must be adept at "people skills." Having more than one boss is often a given in projects. We will present the following topics in this chapter:

1. Communication techniques

2. Factors for developing and maintaining group cohesion

3. Conflict resolution strategies, and

4. Steps for managing effective meetings.

Before presenting guidelines for using these skills, we briefly summarize the stages through which groups and teams evolve. Knowing these steps adds perspective to managing project relations.

EVOLUTION AND TEAM DEVELOPMENT

It is important as a project manager and a team member to realize that newly formed groups and teams go through a development cycle, or stages. The five stages (Kowitz and Knuston, 1980) have been termed

1. Forming stage

2. Storming stage

3. Norming stage

4. Performing stage

5. Adjourning stage

Everyone can expect the *forming stage* to involve team members getting acquainted, "breaking the ice," and starting to build relationships. At the *storming stage* conflict is natural and inevitable. Team members test each other and develop a sense of boundaries and trust. Expect conflict. At the *norming stage*, acceptable unwritten rules and codes of conduct and behavior are developed and shared. Team members know what to expect from each other in working relationships. At the fourth stage, the *performing stage*, the working team is ready to perform. The fifth stage, *adjourning*, is the end of the project or task. Here, the members are dismissed. Celebration occurs and good-byes are said. It is not uncommon for groups to experience elements from previous stages even after they reach this final stage. The goal, however, is to become and maintain a high-performing team.

Communication skills, group cohesiveness, conflict resolution skills, and running effective meetings can enhance your transitions to the performing stage. Be aware of these stages and your development in the team. Aim for the performing stage.

Before presenting communication skills, it is helpful to know the barriers that prevent active listening and feedback. Can you recognize any of these barriers in your communication style?

BARRIERS TO EFFECTIVE COMMUNICATION

Communication in projects is often blocked by barriers which can be avoided if recognized. Most barriers to effective communication are built around judging, sending unwelcome solutions, and avoiding others' concerns.

Robert Bolton (1979) offers these 12 barriers to communication. If observed and remembered, the barriers can be prevented.

JUDGING

1. Criticizing

2. Name-calling

3. Diagnosing

4. Praising/evaluative

SENDING UNWELCOME SOLUTIONS

1. Ordering

2. Threatening

3. Moralizing

4. Excessive/inappropriate questioning

5. Advising

AVOIDING OTHERS' CONCERNS

1. Diverting

2. Logical argument

3. Reassuring

These are straightforward and need no explanation. Remembering and preventing their use is the key to opening communication channels, especially in project situations in which conflict is ongoing. Again, we suggest you use these guidelines for your own effective communication in projects and offer these tips at meetings for others to use. One of the best teachers of effective communication in projects are members who lead by example.

MANAGING COMMUNICATION IN TEAM RELATIONSHIPS

A 3-step process (Bolton, 1979) used for communicating effectively is offered here as a model:

1. Treat the other person with respect.

2. Listen until you "experience the other side."

3. State your views, needs, and feelings assertively, not submissively or aggressively.

Communicating assertively means understanding your own feelings, relating to persons in ways that maintain them and your own self-respect, understanding your rights, and communicating in ways, words, and feelings that get your needs satisfied without hurting, dominating, or abusing the other person's dignity, space, rights, and self-respect (Bolton, 1979). If followed conscientiously and systematically in verbal communication exchanges, this 3-step process can open doors and ideas. Remember it, observe it, use it.

Another set of guidelines to enhance individual and team communication relates to giving and receiving feedback. The following are especially useful in project teams where face-to-face communication involves a great deal of feedback:

Giving feedback should be analogous to holding up a mirror when individuals can see themselves as others see them and learn how their actions have been affecting others. It is *not* telling others what is wrong with them nor telling them how they *should* change. It is offering your perceptions and describing your feelings in a nonjudgmental manner as data that recipients can use as they find appropriate.

1. Examine your own motives.
   Be sure your intention is to be helpful, not to show how perceptive and superior you are, or to hurt the other.

2. Consider the receiver's readiness to hear your feedback.
   In general, feedback is most useful when it is sought, rather than when it is volunteered. When possible, wait for signs of others wanting it; nevertheless,

3. Give feedback promptly.
   Feedback given soon after the event, except when the individual is upset or otherwise not ready to listen, is better than that given when details are no longer in anyone's mind.

4. Be descriptive rather than evaluative.
   Describe what the person did and any feelings it aroused in you, but do not label or evaluate it. ("You interrupted me and that frustrates me because I lose track" is descriptive; "You were rude" is evaluative.)

5. Deal in specifics, not generalities.
   Describe concrete events. ("You interrupted me when I was reviewing . . . " versus "You are trying to hog all the air time.")

6. Offer feedback; do not try to impose it.
   Give information as something the receiver can consider and explore, not as a command that he/she change.

7. Offer feedback in a spirit of tentativeness.
   Offer feedback as one person's perceptions, not a "the truth." Being dogmatic usually puts people on the defensive.

8. Be open to receive feedback yourself.
   Your actions may be contributing to the other's behavior; not everyone may feel the same as you do about the other, which reflects on your perceptions as well as on the other's behavior.

9. Avoid overload.
   Focus only on what is most important and changeable.

10. Watch for behavior of the other while receiving feedback which confirms or disconfirms the behavior. (Cohen et al., 1988, p. 292, reprinted with permission)

Now that you have guidelines for effectively leading, following, communicating, and giving and receiving feedback, we turn to our final topics of

1. increasing group cohesion,

2. resolving conflicts, and

3. running effective meetings.

Remember, the aim is to become and to remain a performing team. This requires "people skills" as well as planning tools.

MANAGING TEAM COHESIVENESS

Creating and managing group cohesiveness is an art and a science. How can we create cohesion in a group or team? Cohen et al. (1988, reprinted with permission) list eight factors that increase cohesion in groups:

1. Required Interactions

   The more frequent the interactions required by the job, the more likely that social relationships and behavior will develop along with task relationships and behavior. The more cohesive the group, the more eager individuals will be for membership, and thus the more likely they will be to confirm to the group's norms. Another way of saying this is: The more cohesive the group, the more influence it has on its members. The less certain and clear a group's norms and standards are, the less control it will have over its members (Festinger et al., 1950; Homans, 1950).

2. Common Attitudes and Goals

   The greater the similarity in member attitudes and values brought to the group, the greater the likelihood of cohesion in a group (Homans, 1950).

3. Superordinate Goal

   Group cohesion will be increased by the existence of a superordinate goal(s) subscribed to by the members (Sherif, 1967).

4. A Common Enemy

   Group cohesion will be increased by the perceived existence of a common enemy (Blake and Mouton, 1961). (Note that this common enemy can be another competitive company, product, or service on the market.)

5. Success in Achieving Goals

   Group cohesion will be increased by success in achieving the group's goals (Sherif and Sherif, 1953). Group cohesion is increased in proportion to the status of the group relative to the other groups in the system (Cartwright and Zander, 1968).

6. Low External Interactions

   Group cohesion will be increased when there is a low frequency of required external interactions (Homans, 1950).

7. Resolution Differences

   The more easily and frequently member differences are settled in a way satisfactory to all members, the greater will be group cohesion (Deutsch, 1968).

8. Availability of Resources

   Group cohesion will increase under conditions of abundant resources. (Cohen et al., 1988, pp. 102–6)

Obviously, not all of these factors will be appropriate all the time, or in every circumstance. It will take practice knowing when to use each one in given circumstances.

The other side of group cohesion is conflict. Every project manager should know strategies for resolving conflicts. The following presentation equips you with problem-solving and conflict-resolution strategies which can help you move beyond stumbling blocks and bottlenecks. These must be read, remembered, practiced, and discussed in your teams.

MANAGING CONFLICT

Six classic steps of collaborative problem solving include:

1. Define the problem in terms of needs, not solutions.
2. Brainstorm possible solutions.
3. Select the solutions that will best meet both party's needs and check possible sequences.
4. Plan who will do what, where, and by when.
5. Implement the plan.
6. Evaluate the problem-solving process and at a later date, how well the solution turned out (Bolton, 1979). The steps are iterative, that is, even though they are sequenced, you can return to any previous step if the process stalls. This approach should be introduced and complemented with the 3-step approach discussed earlier: (1) Treat the other person with respect; (2) listen until you "experience the other side"; and (3) state your views, needs, and feelings assertively, not submissively or aggressively.

Kenneth Thomas (1977, reprinted with permission) offers a range of five different conflict management strategies which we believe can be useful in managing project relationships:

1. Avoiding approaches
2. Accommodating approaches
3. Competing approaches
4. Compromising approaches
5. Collaborating approaches

He also lists the following appropriate conditions for using each of the five strategies. Not every conflict should be accommodated or avoided. Some should be compromised, others collaborated. Here are Thomas's guidelines for handling different types of conflicts.

COMPETING APPROACHES

1. When quick, decisive action is vital.

2. On important issues where unpopular actions need implementing.

3. On issues vital to the organization's welfare, and when you know you are right.

4. Against people who take advantage of noncompetitive behavior.

COLLABORATING APPROACHES

1. To find an integrative solution when both sets of concerns are too important to be compromised.

2. When your objective is to learn.

3. To merge insights from people with different perspectives.

4. To gain commitment by incorporating concerns into a consensus.

5. To work through feelings which have interfered with a relationship.

COMPROMISING APPROACHES

1. When goals are important, but not worth the effort or potential disruption of more assertive modes.

2. When opponents with equal power are committed to mutually exclusive goals.

3. To achieve temporary settlements to complex issues.

4. To arrive at expedient solutions under time pressure.

5. As a backup when collaboration or competition is unsuccessful.

AVOIDING APPROACHES

1. When an issue is trivial or more important issues are pressing.

2. When you perceive no chance of satisfying your concerns.

3. When potential disruption outweighs the benefits of resolution.

4. To let people cool down and regain perspective.

5. When gathering information supersedes immediate decision.

6. When others can resolve the conflict more effectively.

7. When issues seem tangential or symptomatic of other issues.

ACCOMMODATING APPROACHES

1. When you find you are wrong—to allow a better position to be heard, to learn, and to show your reasonableness.

2. When issues are more important to others than to you—to satisfy others and maintain cooperation.

3. To build social credits for later issues.

4. To minimize loss when you are outmatched and losing.

5. When harmony and stability are especially important.

6. To allow subordinates to develop by learning from mistakes.

You may not want to memorize these lists, but you can refer to them daily and note situations in which one strategy or condition requires certain tactics and conflict-resolution methods.

In the following and final section of this chapter, we discuss guidelines for managing effective meetings. Since much of your time as a project manager or team member will be spent in meetings, use these strategies to help your effectiveness and efficiency. Seminar participants and consulting clients tell us that ineffective meetings are a major waste of time in their projects and organizations. This should not be a continuing bad habit.

MANAGING EFFECTIVE MEETINGS

Project meetings will consume more time than any other single activity. It is worth learning and using some effective tips for both running and attending meetings. Let us start by having you ask: Is a meeting necessary? If so, why? If not, what form of information sharing should occur? Could a one-on-one session handle this issue? A letter? A memo? A phone call? If a meeting is necessary, observe these guidelines:

PREPARING FOR THE MEETING

1. Set a few manageable objectives for the meeting. Be brief and keep these simple and action-oriented.

2. Select key participants for the meeting; exclude people who do not need to be present.

3. Select a time and place to meet that satisfies the participants' needs.

4. Prepare and hand out a simple agenda before the meeting. Include points to be addressed, expected or needed outcomes, and follow-up check-points.

RUNNING THE MEETING

1. Begin on time.

2. Have someone take brief key notes and outcomes.

3. Review the agenda with everyone before the meeting concludes.

4. Introduce the participants to each other.

5. Stay with the agenda. Keep on track.

6. Acknowledge everyone's contributions.

7. Conclude by stating the major decisions taken, key outcomes, and details about *follow-up* (who, when, where, and how).

FOLLOW-UP TO THE MEETING

1. Distribute the follow-up agenda to all participants. Highlight the assignments and time/outcome/results sections.

2. Periodically check with persons about their progress and outcomes.

3. Empower people. If there is no enthusiasm, there is no motivation and results will be questionable.

SUMMARY

This chapter provided you with checklists and tips for managing project relationships in order to control project activities effectively. Remember: checklists, guidelines, and tips are only as successful as the commitment and energy people have and bring to a project. Project managers must empower, by example, their teams and other organizational members in order to bring out the excitement and skills of those who work toward meeting the project's goal.

5-PHASE PROJECT MANAGEMENT

| ←————— PLANNING —————→ | ←—————————— IMPLEMENTATION ——————————→ |

1	2	3	4	5
DEFINE	**PLAN**	**ORGANIZE**	**CONTROL**	**CLOSE**
State the Problem	Identify Project Activities	Determine Personnel Needs	Define Management Style	Obtain Client Acceptance
Identify Project Goals	Estimate Time and Cost	Recruit Project Manager	*Establish Control Tools*	Install Deliverables
List the Objectives	Sequence Project Activities	Recruit Project Team	*Prepare Status Reports*	Document the Project
Determine Preliminary Resources	Identify Critical Activities	Organize Project Team	*Review Project Schedule*	Issue the Final Report
Identify Assumptions and Risks	Write Project Proposal	Assign Work Packages	*Issue Change Orders*	Conduct Post-Implementation Audit

| ←———————————————————— DELIVERABLES ————————————————————→ |

• Project Overview	• WBS • Project Network • Critical Path • Project Proposal	• Recruitment Criteria • Work Package Description • Work Package Assignments	• *Variance Reports* • *Status Reports* • *Staff Allocation Reports*	• Final Report • Audit Report

Chapter 9

MAINTAINING THE PROJECT SCHEDULE

Regardless of the extent to which planning was complete and accurate, there will always be a number of events whose outcome could not have been predicted or even controlled. These will always seem to come up at exactly the worst times, will come in threes (as the old saying goes), and will seem to threaten the success of the project. The real "acid test" of your skills as a project manager will be that you were able to detect these problems early enough to take the appropriate corrective action—keeping the project on schedule, within budget, and completed according to specifications.

In this chapter we will identify a number of commonly used reports and control tools aimed at assisting the project manager and activity managers track the progress of the project. We will also illustrate the use of these tools in the Conference Planning Project.

ESTABLISH CONTROL TOOLS

PURPOSE OF CONTROLS

Controls are designed to focus on one or more of the three major components of a project—performance levels, costs, and time schedules. Three reasons for using controls are

1. To track progress

2. To detect variance from plan

3. To take corrective action

To Track Progress

The project manager will want to have in place a periodic (at least monthly) reporting system that identifies the status of every activity in the project. These reports should summarize progress for the current period as well as for the entire project.

To Detect Variance from Plan

In larger projects (say, 50 or more activities) reports that say everything is on schedule and on budget—although music to the ears of the project manager—are too long (and usually too boring) to be read and synthesized. Exception reports, variance reports, and graphical reports provide information for management decision making—and provide it in a concise format. These are discussed below.

To Take Corrective Action

Once a significant variance from plan occurs, the next step is to determine whether corrective action is needed and then act appropriately. In complex projects this will require examining a number of "what ifs." When problems occur in the project, delays result and the project falls behind schedule. For the project to get back on schedule, resources will have to be reallocated. In larger projects the computer will be needed to examine a number of resource reallocation alternatives and pick the best.

PREPARE STATUS REPORTS

In this section we will illustrate, with reports from the Conference Planning Project, examples of reports that track progress, detect variance from the project plan, and suggest corrective actions for getting the project back on schedule. There are three categories of reports that project managers commonly use. Each conveys different information regarding project status. The three reports are variance reports, exception reports, and Gantt Charts.

VARIANCE REPORTING TOOLS

Perhaps one of the simplest reports is the variance report. It provides a snapshot in time (the current period) of the status of the project or any of its activities. It does not report how the project or activity reached that status. That type of reporting is discussed in the section on graphical reporting tools. Variance reports may be used to report project variances (Figure 9-1) or activity variances (Figure 9-2). We recommend that one report format be used to report variances, no matter what the project resource: budget, labor, time, or some other criterion of interest (materials or equipment, for example). Top management will quickly become comfortable with a reporting format that is consistent across all projects or activities within a project. This will reduce the number of questions regarding interpretation or clari-

Figure 9-1   PROJECT VARIANCE REPORT

PROJECT VARIANCE REPORT		Project Name	Project Manager		Date
___ Cost ___ Labor ___ Time ___ Other					

Activity			Budget This Period			Budget To Date		
Number	Name	Manager	Plan	Actual	Var	Plan	Actual	Var
Totals								

Prepared by	Date	Approved by	Date	Sheet ___ of ___

Figure 9-2   ACTIVITY VARIANCE REPORT

ACTIVITY VARIANCE REPORT		Activity Name	Activity Manager	Date
__ Cost __ Labor __ Time __ Other				

Task			Budget This Period			Budget To Date		
Number	Name	Responsibility	Plan	Actual	Var	Plan	Actual	Var
Totals								

Prepared by	Date	Approved by	Date	Sheet ___ of ___

Adapted from Russell D. Archibald. (1976). *Managing High Technology Programs and Projects*. (New York: Wiley), with permission.

fication. It will make life a bit easier for the project manager when it is time to make presentations to top management. For each report period the total resources used (by activity or task within activity) are computed. Comparing these figures against the planned use of resources by computing the variance (planned—actual) provides the project manager with one measure of project status. The same calculations are done for the cumulative actual and planned resource use. Some indication of variance trends can be determined by comparing period variances with cumulative variances, although the graphical reports discussed later give more information on trends in resource use at the activity and project levels.

Positive Variances

Being ahead of schedule or under budget are variances that are music to the ears of the project manager. Positive variances may allow for replanning that will bring the project in ahead of schedule, under budget, or both. If the project manager has multiple project management responsibilities, there may be opportunities to reallocate some resources from projects with positive variances to projects with negative variances.

Negative Variances

Being behind schedule or over budget is not music to the ears of the project manager. This condition may arise for reasons beyond the control of the project manager or project team. Regardless of the reason, the project manager must find ways to correct the situation. In addition to identifying the reason for the variance and correcting it, the manager will need to find ways to reallocate resources from non–critical path activities to those that created the negative variance. The objective will be to bring the project back into agreement with the plan.

In most cases negative time variances will impact project completion only if they are associated with critical path activities. Of lesser concern will be those delays that are associated with non–critical path activities. Whereas less serious variances simply use up some part of the slack time for that activity, more serious ones will cause a change in the critical path.

Negative cost variances may be the result of uncontrollable factors (cost increases from suppliers, increased fuel costs, changes in the tax laws, unexpected equipment malfunctions, etc.). Some may be the result of inefficiencies or error. Whereas every attempt must be made to recover, there may be no alternatives other than budget increases or, alternatively, reduced profit margins.

Figure 9-3 GRAPHICAL VARIATION OF THE VARIANCE REPORT

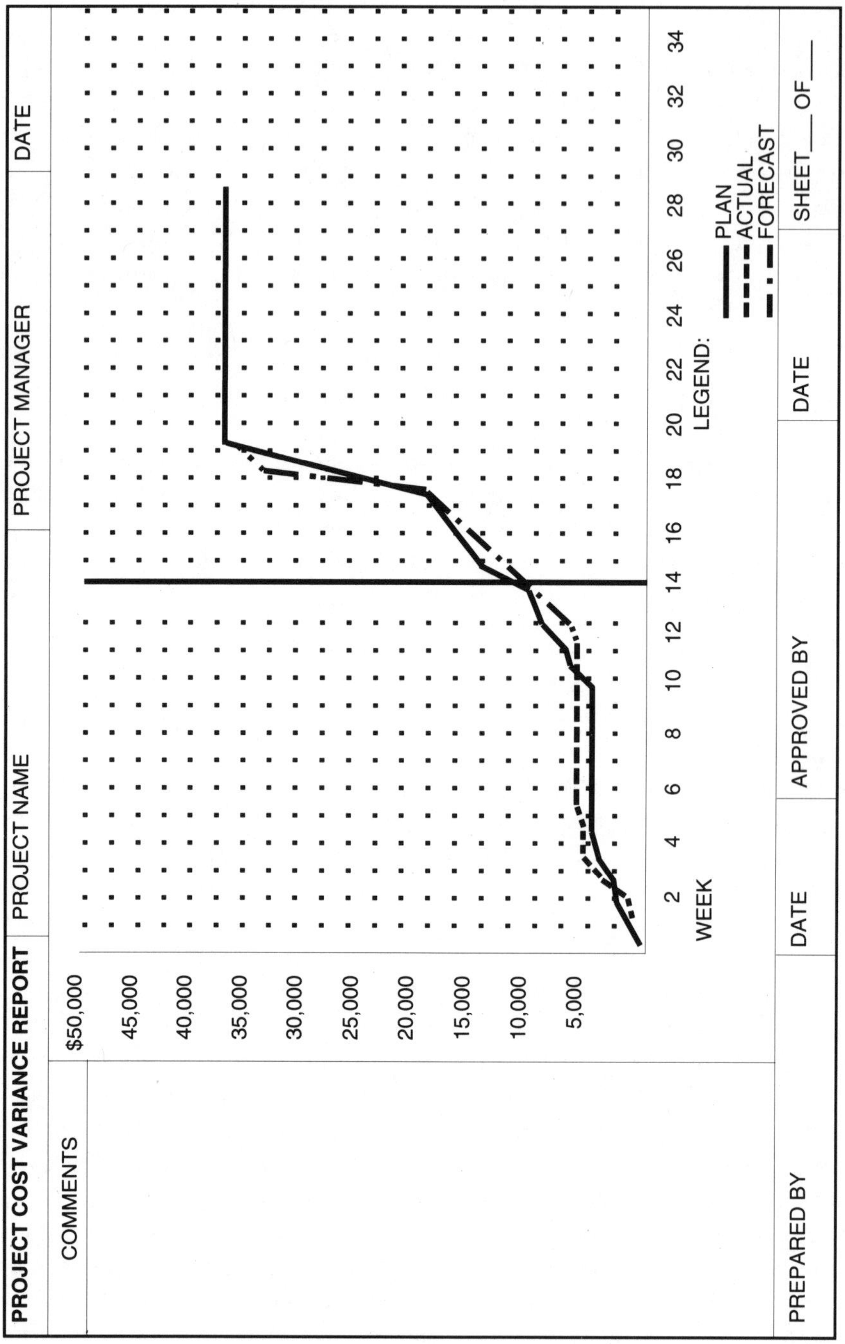

GRAPHICAL REPORTING TOOLS

Managers' time is valuable. To force them to read page after page of data only to conclude that all project activities are on schedule and no intervention on their part is required is to waste their time. A report that identifies actual performance that is outside some nominal (often arbitrarily set) specification is more helpful. For example, the project manager may want to be alerted to any variance that is more than 10 percent above or below plan. In addition, if that condition persists for, say, three consecutive reporting periods, the project manager may also request more detailed reports from the responsible persons in which both the cause and the corrective action is discussed. A simple graphical way to convey that variance from plan information is with cumulative cost or time plots (Figure 9-3). The report date is the end of the 14th week of the project. Cumulative planned expenditures are shown with the solid line, actual expenditures with the dashed line, and the forecasted expenditures for the balance of the project with the alternating dash–dot line. In this case the variance is positive and less has been expended than was planned. Either the project manager has found some economies or the project is behind schedule. When actual expenditures are less than planned it may be the result of being behind schedule and having not yet incurred the expenditures that were planned.

GANTT CHARTS

The cumulative cost variance graph conveys budget information at a glance, but, as we have seen, that does not tell the whole story. By combining it with another graphical report, the Gantt Chart, the actual project status is more easily assessed.

A Gantt Chart is one of the most convenient, most used, and easy-to-grasp depictions of project activities. It is a two-dimensional graphical representation of the activities that comprise the project. The vertical dimension lists the project activities—one per line—while the horizontal dimension is time. Once the scheduled start and completion date of each activity has been determined, the Gantt Chart can be constructed. The value-added of a Gantt Chart is the scaling of project activities according to their duration. This will help put a perspective on the project not obvious in the network representation. On the other hand, the usual representation of a project using the Gantt Chart sacrifices the dependencies between project activities.

Figure 9-4 shows a representation of the Conference Planning Project as a Gantt Chart using a format that we prefer. Over the years we have modified our format of the Gantt Chart to imbed considerable information in one graph. The modifications we have made remove most of the shortcomings attributed to Gantt Charts with little increase in complexity (or clutter). In our format each activity is

Figure 9-4 GANTT CHART SHOWING ASSIGNMENTS AND SCHEDULE USING EARLIEST START TIMES

PROJECT STATUS REPORT		PROJECT NAME	PREPARED BY	DATE	PROJECT MANAGER	APPROVED BY	DATE
NUMBER	NAME	MANAGER					
A	Select Conference Date	Andy					
B	Establish Theme/Program	Beth					
C	Select Conference Site	Andy					
D	Obtain Speakers	Beth					
E	Develop Brochures	Carl					
F	Obtain Mailing Labels	Carl					
G	Mail Brochures	Diane					
H	Obtain Speaker Materials	Beth					
I	Receive Registrations	Diane					
J	Confirm Arrangements	Andy					
K	Prepare Notebooks	Diane					

represented by a bar whose width is the planned time for that activity. One of our · major modifications is to show critical path activities in heavier lined boxes. The precedence relationships are shown with vertical lines connecting the end of the predecessor activity with the beginning of the following activity. Slack time for noncritical activities is shown with dashed lines (this is another of our variations).

Figure 9-5 is the Gantt Chart at the 14th week of the project. The shading shown in the activity bars represents the proportion of that activity that is completed. If the project were exactly on schedule, the shading would extend to the vertical line at the 14th week. Observe that Activities E and F are behind schedule and that Activity H, scheduled to begin in week 16, has already been partially completed. (Perhaps the positive expense variance is the result of Activities E and F being behind schedule.) Activity E is approximately one week behind schedule. Since it is on the critical path, the project manager will want some explanation from Carl as to how he intends to get back on schedule. Activity F is not on the critical path and its 2-week slip from the planned schedule may not be reason for concern at this point.

BALANCE IN THE CONTROL SYSTEM

It is very easy to get carried away with controls and the accompanying reports. Certainly the more controls that are put in place the less likely it will be for the project to get in trouble. The reverse is also true. The fewer the controls the higher the risk of serious problems being detected too late to be resolved. The project manager will need to strike a balance between the extent of the control system and the risk of unfavorable outcomes, just as in the insurance industry where the cost of the policy is compared against the dollar value of the loss that will result from the consequences.

Control also implies rigidity and structure. Both tend to stifle creativity. The project manager will want the team members to have some latitude to exercise their own individuality. The cost of the control must be weighed against the value of empowering team members to be proactive (hence risk takers).

REVIEW PROJECT SCHEDULE

At each milestone the project manager will review from the Status Report provided by each work package manager the status of each work package. Despite all of the planning that went into the project, things will not happen according to plan. Slippages are a fact of life—many are unavoidable and due to inherent variabilities. Some, of course, are due to human error. Here is where project managers

Figure 9-5   STATUS REPORT USING GANTT CHARTS

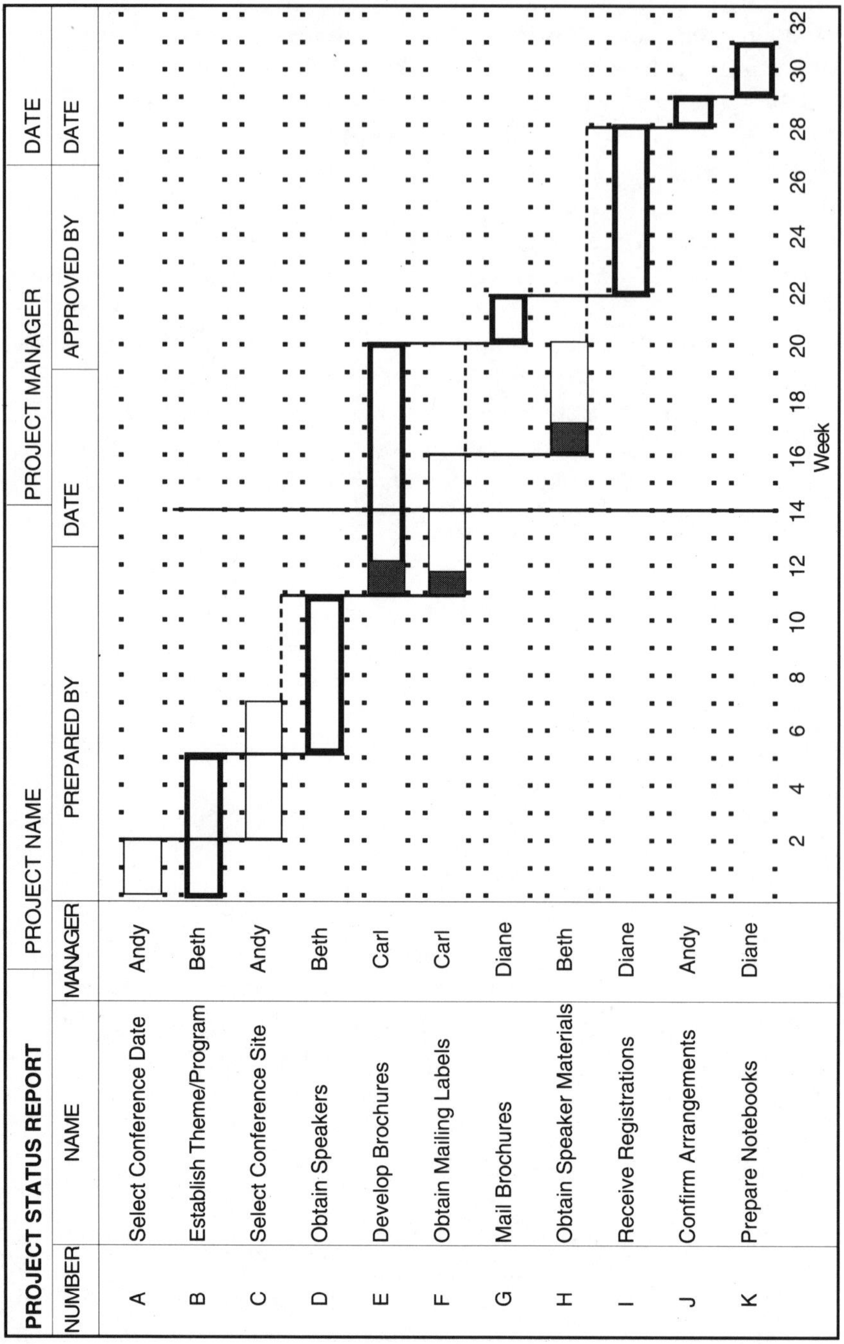

Figure 9-6   PROJECT ACTIVITY SCHEDULE BY TEAM MEMBER

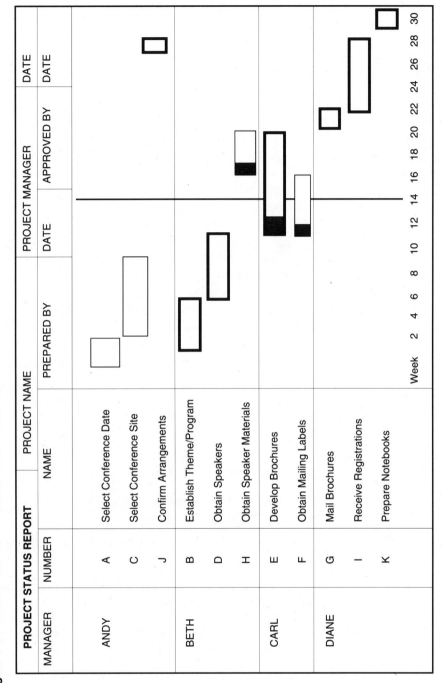

prove their worth: getting back on schedule. For many project managers it may seem that this is all they do.

GETTING BACK ON SCHEDULE

In its simplest form, getting back on schedule involves reallocating resources from non–critical path activities to critical path activities. *Slack management* is a term often used for this task. Figure 9-6 is a report of scheduled activities for each of the project team members. It is simple in form, easy to prepare and update, and contains much of the information that the project manager will need to consider available alternatives. For example, Figure 9-6 is the Status Report at the end of the 14th week of the project. As pointed out in Figure 9-5, Activity E is one week behind schedule and it is a critical path activity. What alternatives might the project manager have to add resources to Activity E, or some later critical path activity, to get the project back on schedule? Looking at Figure 9-6, note that Beth has been able to complete some work on Activity H ahead of schedule and that Activity H is not on the critical path. Beth can be diverted to Activity E (while continuing work on Activity F as time permits) to help Carl get back on schedule. Recall that Activity F does have some slack time but that it must be completed before Activity G (which is on the critical path) can begin. The project manager will be aware of this and can watch at the next milestone for any potential problems.

PROJECT MAINTENANCE QUALITY CONTROL CHECKLIST

YES OR NO

_____ 1. Meaningful reporting frequencies have been established.

_____ 2. The project manager has determined the reporting requirements and informed the work package managers accordingly.

_____ 3. The work package managers understand how to complete each of the required reports.

_____ 4. Variances from plan that will require immediate action have been defined by the project manager and communicated to the project team.

_____ 5. Responsibilities for completing project status reports have been assigned and communicated to the project team and other interested parties.

_____ 6. Top management has been briefed on the reporting procedures and they have been approved.

PROJECT MAINTENANCE ACID TEST

1. The project manager has the appropriate responsibility and authority to complete the project on time, within budget, and according to specifications.

2. The project manager has delegated the appropriate responsibility and authority to the work package managers to complete their work on time, within budget, and according to specifications.

3. The reporting and control system is compatible with that of the organization.

4. The reporting system employed for this project will alert the project team of out-of-control situations early enough to take positive corrective action.

5-PHASE PROJECT MANAGEMENT

←———— PLANNING ————→ ←———————— IMPLEMENTATION ————————→

1	2	3	4	5
DEFINE	**PLAN**	**ORGANIZE**	**CONTROL**	**CLOSE**
State the Problem	Identify Project Activities	Determine Personnel Needs	Define Management Style	*Obtain Client Acceptance*
Identify Project Goals	Estimate Time and Cost	Recruit Project Manager	Establish Control Tools	*Install Deliverables*
List the Objectives	Sequence Project Activities	Recruit Project Team	Prepare Status Reports	*Document the Project*
Determine Preliminary Resources	Identify Critical Activities	Organize Project Team	Review Project Schedule	*Issue the Final Report*
Identify Assumptions and Risks	Write Project Proposal	Assign Work Packages	Issue Change Orders	*Conduct Post-Implementation Audit*

←———————————————— DELIVERABLES ————————————————→

• Project Overview	• WBS • Project Network • Critical Path • Project Proposal	• Recruitment Criteria • Work Package Description • Work Package Assignments	• Variance Reports • Status Reports • Staff Allocation Reports	*• Final Report* *• Audit Report*

Chapter 10

CLOSING THE PROJECT

The project has been planned and implemented. It must now be closed. Who decides when and how the project is to be terminated? Guidelines for a rationale, framework, and process for closing projects are provided here. The end point of the master plan should signal that temporally and from the standpoint of achievement of project goals and deliverables, it is time to terminate the process both formally and informally.

The major phases of project completion include:

- obtaining client acceptance,

- documenting the project,

- conducting the post-implementation audit, and

- issuing the final report.

In this chapter we will discuss steps for accomplishing these phases while terminating the physical operations of the project.

PREPARING TERMINATION LOGISTICS

The rationale for terminating a project is

1. to formally close outside contractual relationships with suppliers, manufacturers, customers, and other budgeted parties who expect an earlier, agreed-upon termination of services;

2. to formally terminate project team member assignments;

3. to obtain client acceptance of the project work and deliverables;

4. to ensure that all deliverables have been installed or implemented according to time, budget, and specifications;

5. to ensure that adequate project documentation and baseline information are in place to facilitate interactions or changes that may need to occur in the future;

6. to issue and obtain sign-off on the final report or status of the project, which shows that the contracted deliverables have been satisfactorily implemented; and

7. to terminate all external and internal relationships.

A post-implementation audit is done and can be added to the final report.

WHO DECIDES TO TERMINATE AND WHEN

A predetermined formal project termination date should have been arranged and signed (even if the first date has been moved) by the project manager and the overseeing administration of the umbrella organization. This close date should agree with the master plan. The project manager initiates the closing of the project with the acknowledgment and cooperation of the administration of the client organization.

THREE TYPES OF PROJECT TERMINATION

Jack Meredith and Samuel Mantel, Jr. (1989) note three types of project termination:

1. by extinction,

2. by inclusion, and

3. by integration.

These three types of termination can help you see how the project is seen by others and how the termination process can take more than one form.

Project termination *by extinction* means the project work as scheduled is either successfully or unsuccessfully done and the decision to terminate is agreed upon. Closing relationships and preparation of the final report must still be completed. This type of termination may cause more stress since the closing is scheduled and the originally planned goals of the project may not have been achieved.

Project termination *by inclusion* means the project is a success and is institutionalized into the organization. This type of termination is seen as a transformation and transitioning process of the project into the larger organization that supported it. The project manager must take special care to ensure a smooth transition.

Project termination *by integration* is the most common way of closing successful projects. It is also the most complex. Project equipment, material, and personnel must be distributed back into the parent organization. Unlike termination by inclusion, the project may not be seen as a competitor when resources are integrated. The work of the project manager is significant in all three types of terminations. Knowing at the outset of the project which type of termination may likely occur can help you plan the operations for inclusion or integration.

CHECKLIST FOR TERMINATION

The following checklist (Meredith and Mantel, 1989) serves as a guide which can assist you in determining the readiness of the project for termination apart from published or planned dates and deadlines:

1. Is the project still consistent with organizational goals?

2. Is it practical? Useful?

3. Is management sufficiently enthusiastic about the project to support its implementation?

4. Is the scope of the project consistent with the organization's financial strength?

5. Is the project consistent with the notion of a "balanced" program in all areas of the organization's technical interests? In "age"? In cost?

6. Does the project have the support of all the departments (e.g., finance, manufacturing, marketing, etc.) needed to implement it?

7. Is organizational project support being spread too thin?

8. Is support of this individual project sufficient for success?

9. Does this project represent too great an advance over current technology? Too small an advance?

10. Is this project team still innovative? Has it gone stale?

11. Can the new knowledge be protected by patent, copyright, or trade secret?

12. Could this project be farmed out without loss of quality?

13. Is the current project team properly qualified to continue the project?

14. Does the organization have the required skills to achieve full implementation or exploitation of the project?

15. Has the subject area of the project already been "thoroughly plowed"?

16. Has the project lost its key person or champion?

17. Is the project team enthusiastic about success?

18. Would the potential results be more efficiently developed in-house than purchased or subcontracted outside?

19. Does it seem likely that the project will achieve the minimum goals set for it? Is it still profitable? Timely?

Whatever form the termination takes, the project manager still needs a termination process to structure and implement the project's close. Once all the checklist items have been addressed, steps for the termination can begin.

PROJECT TERMINATION PROCESS

The termination process can be as complicated and lengthy as the size, complexity, and scope of the project itself. A systematic process is therefore needed to assist the project manager in successfully covering all bases in order to terminate contracts and relationships. The general termination phases are illustrated in Figure 10-1. These phases include:

1. prepare termination logistics,

2. document the project,

3. conduct post-implementation audit and prepare and submit final report,

4. obtain client approval, and, finally,

5. close operations.

The following steps, as represented in Figure 10-2, are recommended to help you structure a process that meets your specific project needs:

1. Establish a project termination design to organizationally close the project:

    (a) Assign a termination manager.

    (b) Assign a termination team to assist the manager.

2. Conduct a termination meeting to review this process. Make close-out assignments.

3. Prepare project personnel termination reports. Close down project office and reporting systems.

Figure 10-1   PHASES OF PROJECT TERMINATION

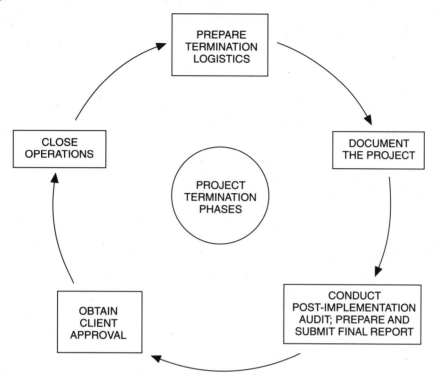

4. Terminate all financial documents; complete all payments and expenses; collect all debts; prepare the financial project closing report.

5. Terminate all work orders, contracts, assignments, and outstanding supplier and customer obligations.

6. Document completion and compliance with all vendors and contractors.

7. Close all project sites and return all project equipment.

8. Conduct and complete post-implementation audit. Complete final report. Submit to client.

9. Obtain client's approval.

10. Close all physical sites and terminate remaining project staff.

Stay close to the client and the administration of the supporting organization throughout this process. Your close-down is dependent on client satisfaction and the quality of the services the project provided.

Figure 10-2 TERMINATION PROCESS

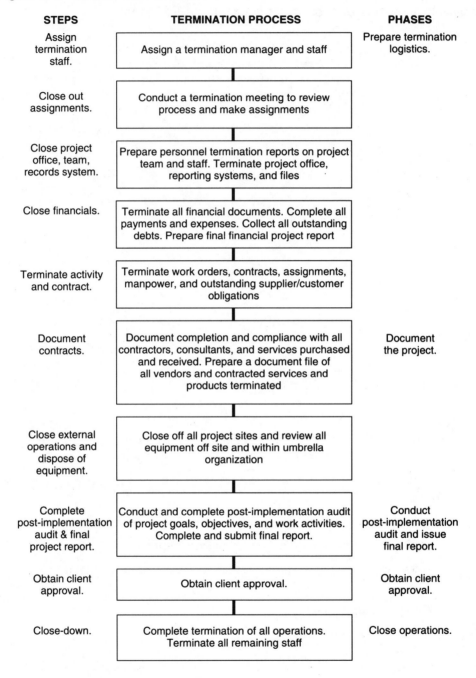

STEPS	TERMINATION PROCESS	PHASES
Assign termination staff.	Assign a termination manager and staff	Prepare termination logistics.
Close out assignments.	Conduct a termination meeting to review process and make assignments	
Close project office, team, records system.	Prepare personnel termination reports on project team and staff. Terminate project office, reporting systems, and files	
Close financials.	Terminate all financial documents. Complete all payments and expenses. Collect all outstanding debts. Prepare final financial project report	
Terminate activity and contract.	Terminate work orders, contracts, assignments, manpower, and outstanding supplier/customer obligations	
Document contracts.	Document completion and compliance with all contractors, consultants, and services purchased and received. Prepare a document file of all vendors and contracted services and products terminated	Document the project.
Close external operations and dispose of equipment.	Close off all project sites and review all equipment off site and within umbrella organization	
Complete post-implementation audit & final project report.	Conduct and complete post-implementation audit of project goals, objectives, and work activities. Complete and submit final report.	Conduct post-implementation audit and issue final report.
Obtain client approval.	Obtain client approval.	Obtain client approval.
Close-down.	Complete termination of all operations. Terminate all remaining staff	Close operations.

Source: Adapted from Jack R. Meredith and Samuel J. Mantel, Jr. (1989), *Project Management: A Managerial Approach,* 2d ed. (New York: Wiley), chap. 4, with permission.

POST-IMPLEMENTATION AND FINAL PROJECT REPORT

The post-implementation audit is an evaluation of the project's goals and activity achievement as measured against the project plan, budget, time deadlines, quality of deliverables, specifications, and client satisfaction. The log of the project activities serves as baseline data for this audit. The driving questions include:

1. Was the project goal achieved?

2. Was project work done on time, was it done within budget, and was it done by specifications?

3. Was the client satisfied with the project results?

The Final Project Report serves as the memory or history of the project. It is the file that others can check to study the progress and impediments of the project. There are many formats that can be used for a final report. The following elements are usually included:

- Overall success and performance of the project (using the post-implementation audit results)

- Organization and administration of the project

- Techniques used to accomplish project results

- Assessment of project strengths and weaknesses

- Recommendations from the project manager and team for continuation or extinction of the project

REWARDING THE SUCCESSES, LEARNING FROM THE FAILURES

Closing the project with a celebration of the effort as well as the results brings resolution to the process. The project manager's last effort is to bring the team together to review their journey. This is a way of closing informal as well as formal relationships. Not all projects terminate on an upbeat note. Still, a great deal of learning has occurred. A final meeting, party, dinner, or gala brings the project life cycle full circle.

Part III

PROJECT MANAGEMENT FOR THE 21ST CENTURY

Project management methods continue to be popular and useful tools in organizations. As we approach the 21st century, we notice several changes which managers must consider in planning and implementing projects: an increased customer focus; managing multiple projects, or "program management"; using a "stakeholder analysis" to plan and implement projects; and use of horizontal task forces. The epilogue which follows highlights these trends.

Epilogue

CONTEMPORARY ISSUES IN PROJECT MANAGEMENT

CUSTOMER FOCUS

Whether the end user of the project is a department or business unit in the organization or the purchaser of the organization's products or services, the trend in successful organizations is to have them involved in the project. We have continually stressed the need for buy-in of the project's end user. The importance of this is even more evident in projects that involve the development of software systems and products. Among the most progressive organizations it is not unusual to find the end user in the role of project manager. This places added responsibility on the shoulders of the systems and programming staff, especially on the systems analysts who serve on the project team.

It also places added responsibility on the shoulders of the end user department. The project was approved because of favorable cost/benefit ratios. It will be the responsibility of the end user to demonstrate that those benefits have indeed been realized.

PROGRAM MANAGEMENT

Projects whose activities are themselves projects are called programs. A detailed discussion of program management is beyond the scope of this book. Still, many of the techniques we have discussed are relevant.

The program manager will, of course, have to face an additional layer of complexity. This is most evident when resources must be shared across several projects. A good example of this is the systems development unit in the information systems department. The analysts and programmers will most likely have responsibilities in multiple projects, either in one program or across several programs.

Compared to projects, programs will be of longer duration. This adds another complexity usually not found in projects—staff turnover. Program managers will have to pay more attention to staff hiring, training, and development. The program network will have to include activities related to program team development. These activities, even if nothing more than contingency plans, will still have to be budgeted and managed effectively to ensure that the human resources are available when needed.

STAKEHOLDER ANALYSIS

The Stakeholder Analysis (Freeman, 1983; Weiss, 1991) is another strategic tool project managers can use to map and understand planned obligations and tactics when dealing with dispersed customers, suppliers, competitors, government bodies, and external groups. The Stakeholder Analysis is not new. As used here, it simply maps different groups that have a stake or interest in the project.

The purposes of the analysis are

1. to enable the project manager to identify the groups that must be interacted with to accomplish project goals;

2. to develop strategies and tactics to effectively negotiate competing goals and interests among the different groups;

3. to identify strategic interests each group has in the project in order to negotiate common interests; and

4. to help the project manager better allocate resources to deal with these different constituencies in order to accomplish project goals.

Many projects are extremely complex and require a number of external interactions for completion. The Stakeholder Analysis simplifies the complexity. The project manager can assess external resources and threats and strategically plan appropriate responses.

ORGANIZATIONAL CHANGES

There are dramatic, even revolutionary, changes now taking place in the corporate world which are affecting the way projects are managed. The rapid emergence of software useful to even the unsophisticated and the realization that information systems can dramatically impact the organization's competitive position have resulted in both vertical and horizontal changes in the structure and operation of organizations. Specifically, project teams are formed along temporary, "dotted-line" reporting relationships to other organizational managers; project teams are formed as part of "ad hocracies," that is, organizational units with *ad hoc* objectives; and project teams may be part of emerging network organizations, that is, splintered units that out-source products, goods, and services. As organizations continue to "blur" their boundaries, project teams will increase in importance because teams can be used to pull and combine resources across functional areas and even geographies.

VERTICAL THINNING

Because of the computer, information is more accessible to managers at all levels in the organization; therefore, the need for layer upon layer of middle managers is being questioned. In many organizations it has been concluded that several layers of management exist primarily to interpret information and pass it up or down to the next level of management. Access to information has become so easy that many managers can query the system directly rather than work through intermediaries. In that sense use of several layers of management has become obsolete and they have in fact been removed in many organizations. There are also strong indications that even clerical support staff are disappearing as many managers can now do much of their own word processing and use electronic mail to communicate what once had to be communicated through an endless stream of memos.

For the project manager computers and easy access to information is both good news and bad news. The good news is that there is now a much better set of tools to monitor and report project status, to detect out-of-control situations, and to evaluate and even suggest alternative solutions. The bad news is that top management can also directly monitor project progress. Project managers will be put to the task; not only must they stay current with project activity, they must also be prepared to respond quickly and be ready with answers to questions that top management will now be able to ask.

HORIZONTAL TASK FORCES

Peter Drucker, writing in the *Harvard Business Review* in January–February 1987, spoke of the coming of a new organization—one whose structure is nothing more than a loose federation of task forces. Each task force contains all the expertise it needs to carry out its mission. If such is to be—and there is sufficient evidence to support Drucker's claim—then here is where the rubber will meet the road as far as project management is concerned. Task managers (a.k.a. project managers) will have one or more projects under their control. They will also have sufficient autonomy (and the requisite responsibility) to make day-to-day decisions and manage the affairs of their projects. They will be responsible not only for bringing the project in on time, within budget, and according to specifications, but also for developing their team to function effectively on more than one project.

The simple, quick, and effective tools we have shown here will be indispensable for working in the changing environment of organizations. Certainly one can envision much more complex and detailed tools and documentation—and many have—but we believe that our simple approach will be best for most of the projects you may encounter.

Appendix

PROJECT MANAGEMENT SOFTWARE

For those interested in using one of the many software packages available for both mainframe and micro-computer environments, we advise checking one of the more popular evaluation sources first. Two that regularly publish such reviews are

> Project Management Institute
> P. O. Box 43
> Drexel Hill, PA 19026
> (415) 622–1796
>
> and
>
> Software Digest
> One Winding Drive
> Philadelphia, PA 19131–2903
> 1–800–223–7093 (in PA 1–800–222–3315)

InfoWorld periodically publishes evaluations of project management packages. The most recent evaluation appeared in November 1990. In that review they evaluated Harvard Project Manager, Instaplan 5000, Microsoft Project for Windows, Project Scheduler 5, Superproject Expert, and Time Line. There is no single package that is considered best. As in all software selection decisions it is important to first specify the functionality that your situation requires and then find the package that meets that criteria. Cost ($495 to $20,000 and more), hardware environment, single user or networked, and perhaps other constraints may further limit your choices.

As you look for the appropriate software package, ease-of-use should be a "non-negotiable." An easy trap to fall into is to become enamored with the glitz and glitter of the package and forget about the overhead. When the number of activities in the project grows to 50 or more, any serious project management effort will have to include a software package. Industry surveys, software reviews, and user evaluations will be indispensable in deciding which package best meets your needs.

Bibliography and Cited References

Adams, Everett, Jr., and Ronald J. Ebert (1978). *Production and Operations Management* (Englewood Cliffs, NJ: Prentice-Hall).

Archibald, Russell (1976). *Managing High-Technology Programs and Projects* (New York: Wiley).

Awani, Alfred (1983). *Project Management Techniques* (New York: Petroteil Books), chap. 10.

Bacon, J. (1970). *Managing the Budget Function* (New York: National Industrial Conference Board).

Balachandra, R. and J. A. Raelin (1980). "How to Decide When to Abandon a Project." *Research Management*, July, pp. 24–29.

Bander, Diana (1986). "Building a Better Project Manager." *Computerworld*, May 26, pp. 69–74.

Bartizal, J. R. (1940). *Budget Principles and Procedures* (Englewood Cliffs, NJ: Prentice-Hall).

Bienkowski, Danek (1989). "Ten Causes of Project Busts." *Computerworld*, February 13, p. 99.

Blake, R. and J. Mouton (1961). "Reactions to Intergroup Competition Under Win–Lose Competition." *Management Science*, July, pp. 420–25.

Block, R. (1983). *The Politics of Projects* (New York: Yourdon Press).

Bolton, Robert (1979). *People Skills* (Englewood Cliffs, NJ: Prentice-Hall).

Burman, J. (1972). *Precedence Networks for Project Planning and Control* (New York: McGraw-Hill).

Cartwright, D. and Z. Zander (Eds.) (1968). *Group Dynamics: Research and Theory* (New York: Harper & Row).

Cleland, D. I. and W. R. King (Eds.) (1983). *Project Management Handbook* (New York: Van Nostrand Reinhold).

Clifton, D. S. (1975). *Project Feasibility Analysis* (New York: Wiley).

Cohen, Allan R., Fink, Stephen, Gadon, Herman, Willits, Robin, with the collaboration of Natasha Josefowitz (1988). *Effective Behavior in Organizations*, 4th ed. (Homewood, IL: Irwin).

Cooke, Terry-Davies (1990). "Return of the Project Managers." *Management Today*, May 1990, pp. 119–20.

Corcoran, Elizabeth (1990). "Computer Babble: Manufacturers Move Slowly to Adopt Open Systems." *Scientific American,* January, pp. 100–102.

Covey, Stephen R. (1989). *The 7 Habits of Highly Effective People* (New York: Simon and Schuster).

DeMarco, T. (1982). *Controlling Software Projects* (New York: Yourdon Press).

Deutsch, M. (1968). "The Effects of Cooperation and Competition upon Group Success." In D. Cartwright and Z. Zander (Eds.), *Group Dynamics: Research and Theory* (New York: Harper & Row).

Dilworth, B. James, Robert C. Ford, Peter M. Ginter, and Andrew C. Rucks (1985). "Centralized Project Management." *Journal of Systems Management,* August, pp. 30–35.

Doran, George T. (1981). "There's a S.M.A.R.T. Way to Write Management Goals and Objectives." *Management Review,* November, pp. 35–36.

Doughty, Rick and Ralph Kliem (1987). "Making Software Engineering Project Managers Successful." *Journal of Systems Management,* September, pp. 18–23.

Doyle, M. and D. Straus (1977). *How to Make Meetings Work* (New York: Harper & Row).

Dressler, Donna M. (1986). "In Project Management, the Emphasis Should Be on Management." *Data Management,* January, p. 62.

Drucker, Peter (1987). "The Coming of the New Organization." *Harvard Business Review,* January–February, pp. 45–53.

Dyer, William (1987). *Team Building, Issues and Alternatives,* 2d ed., (Reading, MA: Addison-Wesley).

Festinger, L., S. Schachter, and K. Back (1950). *Social Pressures in Informal Groups: A Study of Human Factors in Housing* (New York: Harper & Row).

Fleming, Mary M. K. (1986). "Keys to Successful Project Management." *CMA Magazine,* November–December, pp. 58–61.

Frame, J. Davidson (1987). *Managing Projects in Organizations* (San Francisco: Jossey-Bass).

Frame, J. D. (1969). *Managing Projects in Organizations, How to Make the Best Use of Time, Technique, and People* (San Francisco: Jossey-Bass).

Freedman, D. P. and G. M. Weinberg (1982). *Handbook of Walkthroughs, Inspections, and Technical Reviews,* 3d ed. (Boston: Little, Brown).

Freeman, R. Edward (1983). *Strategic Management: A Stakeholders Approach* (Boston: Pittman).

Gilbreath, R. D. (1986). *Winning at Project Management: What Works, What Fails, and Why* (New York: Wiley).

Hajek, V. G. (1984). *Management of Engineering Projects* (New York: Wiley).

Harrison, F. L. (1984). *Advanced Project Management* (New York: Wiley).

Hoare, H. R. (1973). *Project Management Using Network Analysis* (New York: McGraw-Hill).

Homans, G. C. (1950). *The Human Group* (New York: Harcourt Brace Jovanovich).

House, Ruth Sizemore (1988). *The Human Side of Project Management* (Reading, MA: Addison-Wesley), chaps. 5 and 6.

Hover, L. D. (1979). *A Practical Guide to Budgeting and Management Control Systems: A Functional and Performance Evaluation Approach* (Lexington, MA: Lexington Books).

Kanter, Elizabeth R. (1989). *When Giants Learn to Dance: Mastering the Challenge of Strategy, Management and Careers in the 1990's* (New York: Simon and Schuster).

Kerzner, Harold (1982). *Project Management for Executives* (New York: Van Nostrand Reinhold).

Kerzner, Harold (1979). *Project Management: A Systems Approach to Planning, Scheduling and Controlling* (New York: Van Nostrand Reinhold).

Khalil, T. and B. Bayraktar (Eds.) (1990). *Management of Technology II: The Key to Global Competitiveness* (Norcross, GA: Industrial Engineering and Management Press).

Kidder, Tracy (1981). *The Soul of a New Machine* (New York: Avon Books).

Kowitz, A. C. and T. J. Knuston (1980). *Decision Making in Small Groups: The Search for Alternatives* (Boston: Allyn and Bacon).

Lee, S. M., Moeller, Gerald L., and Lester A. Graham (1982). *Network Analysis for Management Decisions* (Boston: Kluner Nijhoff).

Lin, T. (1979). "Corporate Planning and Budgeting: An Integrated Approach." *Managerial Planning,* May, pp. 29–33.

Maidique, Modesto and Robert Hayes (1984). "The Art of High-Technology Management." *Sloan Management Review,* Winter, pp. 17–31.

Margin, O. C. (1976). *Project Management* (New York: AMACOM Books).

Menkus, Belden (1987). "There Are Many Reasons Why Some Systems Projects Are Unsuccessful." *Journal of Systems Management,* September, p. 5.

Meredith, Jack R. and Samuel J. Mantel, Jr. (1989). *Project Management: A Managerial Approach* (New York: Wiley), chap. 4.

Meyer, John R. and James M. Gustafson (Eds.) (1988). *The U.S. Business Corporation: An Institution in Transition* (Cambridge, MA: Ballinger).

Mintzberg, Henry (1973). *The Nature of Managerial Work* (New York: Harper & Row), pp. 92–93.

Mishan, E. J. (1982). *Cost Benefit Analysis,* 3d ed. (Winchester, MA: Allen and Unwin).

Moder, J. J. (1983). *Project Management with CPM, PERT, and Precedence Diagramming* (New York: Van Nostrand Reinhold).

Moriarty, Rowland and Thomas Kosnik (1989). "High-Tech Marketing: Concepts, Continuity and Change." *Sloan Management Review,* Summer, pp. 7–17.

Norko, W. A. (1986). "Steps to Successful Project Management." *Journal of Systems Management*, September, pp. 36–38.

Page-Jones, M. (1985). *Practical Project Management: Restoring Quality to DP Projects and Systems* (New York: Dorset House).

Parmar Lakhbir (1987). "Success Factors in Managing Systems Projects." *Data Management*, p. 27.

Peters, Thomas J. and Robert H. Waterman, Jr. (1982). *In Search of Excellence* (New York: Harper & Row).

Pinto, Jeffrey K. and Dennis P. Slevin (1989). "The Project Champion: Key to Implementation Success." *Project Management Journal*, December, pp. 15–20.

Pinto, Jeffrey K. and Dennis P. Slevin (1987). "Critical Factors in Successful Project Implementation." *IEEE Transactions of Engineering Management*, February, pp. 22–27.

Randolph, A. and B. Posner (1988). *Effective Project Planning & Management, Getting the Job Done* (Englewood Cliffs, NJ: Prentice-Hall).

Raudsepp, Eugene (1987). In R. L. Kuhn (Ed.), *Handbook for Creative Managers* (New York: McGraw-Hill), pp. 173–82.

Ruskin, A. M. and W. E. Estes (1985). "The Project Management Audit: Its Role and Conduct." *Project Management Journal*, August, pp. 64–70.

Russell, Archibald (1976). *Managing High Technology Programs and Projects* (New York: Wiley).

Russo, W. M. and R. T. Greenway (1990). "A Framework for Managing Enterprise-Wide Information Systems Technology." In T. Khalil and B. Bayraktar (Eds.), *Management of Technology II: Proceedings of the Second International Conference on Management of Technology* (Norcross, GA: Industrial Engineering and Management Press), pp. 983–92.

Salinger, Anthony W. (1985). "Leadership, Communication Skills Lift Projects to Success." *Data Management*, September, pp. 36–37.

Sherif, M. (1967). *Group Conflict and Cooperation: Their Social Psychology* (Boston: Routledge and Kegan Paul).

Sherif, M. and C. Sherif (1953). *Groups in Harmony and Tension* (New York: Harper & Row).

Silverman, M. (1976). *Project Management: A Short Course for Professionals* (New York: Wiley).

Spinner, M. (1981). *Elements of Project Management* (Englewood Cliffs, NJ: Prentice-Hall).

Stewart, John M. (1965). "Making Project Management Work." *Business Horizons*, Fall, pp. 54–68.

Stuckebruck, C. (Ed.) (1981). *The Implementation of Project Management: The Professional's Handbook* (Reading, MA: Addison-Wesley).

Thomas, Kenneth W. (1977). "Toward Multi-dimensional Values in Teaching: The Example of Conflict Behaviors." *Academy of Management Review* 2, No. 3, p. 487.

Thomsett, R. (1980). *People & Project Management* (New York: Yourdon Press).

Turner, W. S. III (1980). *Project Auditing Methodology* (Amsterdam: North Holland).

Webber, Ross A. (1975). *Management* (Homewood, IL: Irwin).

Weiss, Joseph W. (1991). "Computer Firms and Global Competitiveness in the 1990's: Implementation of Total Solutions Enterprise Strategies." *Business and the Contemporary World,* May, pp. 113–20. Bentley College, Waltham, MA.

Weiss, Joseph W. (1990). "Enterprise Program Management Methodology: Computer Firms Map to the 1990's." Unpublished paper, Bentley College, Department of Management, Waltham, MA.

Weiss, Joseph W. and Hans J. Thamhain (1992). "Project Management: Strategic and Competitive Uses in Twenty High Technology Companies." Paper delivered at the Third International Conference on the Management of Technology, Feb. 17–21, University of Miami, Miami, FL.

Weist, J. D. and F. Levey (1977). *A Management Guide to PERT/CPM,* 2d ed. (Englewood Cliffs, NJ: Prentice-Hall).

Zeldman, M. (1978). *Keeping Technical Projects on Target* (New York: AMACOM Books).

Index